TRAINING FOR GOLD: THE PLAN THAT MADE DANIEL STÅHL AN OLYMPIC CHAMPION

Vésteinn Hafsteinsson

With Dan McQuaid

GLOBAL THROWING

Acknowledgments

We owe thanks to many.

First, to Hans Üürike and the late Shaun Pickering for providing the impetus to get this project moving.

To Roger Einbecker, who, besides taking on all the technical aspects of turning a lot of stories and numbers into a book, was a calm and reassuring presence through these last crazy two-and-a-half years, though he could never keep his dogs quiet during Zooms.

To our wives, Anna Hafsteinsson Östenberg, Alice Wood, and Nancy Einbecker, for their support and encouragement and for pretending not to miss us during the hours we spent sequestered in Zoomland working on this project.

To Mike McQuaid for help with the design.

And, to Arwid Koskinen for the fantastic cover photo.

Contents

Acknowledgments 1
Introduction 3
2020-2021 Detailed Training Plan 9
   First Yellow Period - 5th October to 20th December 2020 12
      5th October to 11th October (Program 1 Base 1) 12
      26th October to 1st November (Program 2 Base 2) 17
      23rd November to 29th November (Program 3 Base 3) 26
   Red Period - 21st December 2020 to 3rd January 2021 33
   First Green Period - 4th January to 7th February 2021 34
      1st February to 7th February 2021 (Program 5 Strength 1) 34
   First Blue Period – 15th February to 7th March 2021 39
      15th February to 21st February (Program 7 Power & Speed 1) 39
   Second Yellow Period – 15th March to 29th May 2021 46
      Beginning Weeks: 15th March to 4th April (Program 9 Base 4) 47
      Middle Weeks: 5th April to 2nd May 50
      5th April to 11th April (Program 10 Base 5) 50
   Second Yellow Period Final Segment: 3rd May to 29th May 58
      3rd May to 12th May (Program 11 Base 6) 58
   Second Green Period - 30th May to 13th July 2021 64
   Second Blue Period - Fukuoka, July 14-31, 2021 93
Afterward 115
About the Authors 116

Introduction

I learned many lessons about training over the years. The first came when my childhood friend Óskar Reykdalsson decided he wanted to be the best shot putter in the world.

Óskar and I grew up in the small town of Selfoss, Iceland, during a time when there was not much else for kids to do except play sports. Iceland had only one television channel then, and most people couldn't afford to own a TV anyway. If we kids wanted to watch a show, we would stand on the sidewalk in front of a local store and look through the window at the TVs they were selling. But it was too cold in Iceland to stand still for long, and so we played sports. All the sports. Selfoss might have been small, but every kid had a chance to try soccer, golf, basketball, handball, swimming and of course, athletics—or, as the Americans call it, track and field.

In the summer, the Icelandic Federation hosted meets in Reykjavik where top guys like future European Indoor shot put champion Hreinn Halldórsson would compete. Óskar Jakobsson, who ended up making the Olympics in the shot, discus, and javelin, also threw in those Reykjavik meets. And so did my friend Óskar and I. Everyone was welcome. We would ride the bus from Selfoss, compete, take in one film at a movie theater, get back on the bus and arrive home at 12:00 a.m. when there was still light because of the midnight sun. We were thirteen years old then.

That summer, Óskar fell in love with the shot put and so had no choice but to try to become the world's best at it.

In order to achieve this, he decided he must train twice per day.

I asked him how he would do it, since school began at 8:15 a.m. and we usually had practices for our other sports, like soccer and basketball, in the afternoons and evenings.

"I don't know what you're going to do," he said. "But I'm going to get up early before school and run."

At that point in our lives, we had no idea what it meant to train for the shot put. To us, training was training, so five times a week, Óskar got up at 6:00 a.m. to run in the streets of Selfoss, and I got up to run with him.

Óskar was heavier and slower than me, so after a while, I got bored running at his pace. But I liked the feeling of doing something special every day, something extra that most people were not willing to do. So, I still showed up every morning. I just ran at my own speed, waving to Óskar whenever we crossed paths.

Those morning runs gave me my first lessons in discipline.

More lessons came when my father, Hafsteinn Þorvaldsson (Thorvaldson), who was president of the athletics club system in all of Iceland except Reykjavik, brought a coach from Denmark named Ole Schöler to work with our club in Selfoss. Ole's leadership changed my life. He got me to understand that in order to be the best, I must not only train hard but also study to learn how the body and mind work. Under Ole's guidance, Óskar and I continued to train twice per day, but now instead of running we would do technical drills and plyometrics. He also started us on a weightlifting program.

At the time, not many people understood the benefits of weight training for athletes. My brother, Þráinn (Thrain) Hafsteinsson, who also had a big influence on my development as an athlete and coach, was one, and Ole was another.

In those days, the people who lifted weights in Selfoss were not athletes. They were the local tough guys who drove around town in Chevy Impalas trying to get attention from the girls. The tough guys suspected that having big muscles might also impress the girls, so they asked permission to put some bars and plates into the basement of the swimming hall, and that is where Óskar and I went to train. It was a terrible place, hot and damp with leaky pipes hanging from the ceiling so low you could barely do a snatch or jerk! The tough guys brought in some old couches for their friends and girlfriends to sit on, and their little weightroom was often full of people in tattoos and leather jackets, smoking and drinking vodka while we lifted. The tough guys trained in short shorts or sometimes just in their underwear, with knee-high socks and John Travolta shoes, the kind with thick soles and high heels popular in the 1970s. Nobody in my family ever smoked, drank alcohol, or wore Travolta shoes, so all of this was new to me.

After a while, the lifters got kicked out of the swimming hall, so they moved their "gym" to an old car repair shop which was about to be torn down. It had broken windows and no heat, oil on the floor and mice running around, but again it was our only choice if we wanted to train with weights. Eventually, the lifters got thrown out of the repair shop as well and set up in a small building the bus company owned which was also scheduled to be demolished.

Training with the tough guys gave Óskar and me more practice in commitment and discipline. It was not comfortable for us to lift weights in cramped rooms full of cigarette smoke and guys wearing disco shoes, but we had gotten it in our heads that we wanted to be the best, so we made no excuses and never missed a session.

Ole required us to submit regular written reports to him about our lifting and did his best to teach us the scientific basis of training.

He also worked to help us improve our mental strength. Sometimes, he would bring the athletes in our club together to put on a play with only ten minutes of rehearsal. This was his way of teaching us to stay calm under pressure. I didn't understand everything he did at the time, but now I am grateful, and I thank him for the coach I became.

I continued lifting when I went to high school in Reykjavik, and the weight room there was even crazier than in Selfoss. It was located in an old laundromat, and some serious Olympic and powerlifters trained there, guys who seemed like they were double as big as me. They would come from their factory jobs and prepare for lifting by walking around the gym smoking, drinking Coca-Cola, and slowly stripping off their work clothes until they were down to their underwear just like the tough guys in Selfoss. Jón Páll Sigmarsson was one of them. Later, he won the World's Strongest Man title four times. One day in the Reykjavik gym he wrote on the wall, "I will not be with a woman until I break the European record in the deadlift." I do not know if Jón Páll kept his vow, but he did end up breaking the record.

The guys in those crazy gyms in Selfoss and Reykjavik taught me a lot about weightlifting.

Another important learning experience from this time was when I got a copy of the book *Wilkins vs. Powell: A Comparative Study* by Ernie Bullard and Larry Knuth. Mac Wilkins and John Powell were the best discus throwers in the world then and I wanted to learn their secrets, so I sat down with an English-Icelandic dictionary and made a translation.

From that book, I learned much of the philosophy I later used during my coaching career. Be patient. Believe in yourself. Strive to reach your potential. Compete against yourself. These are all concepts I preached to my athletes over the years, and they came from reading *Wilkins vs. Powell* when I was a teenager.

I competed in the decathlon for a few years when I was in high school, but by 1979 I decided my future was in the discus. Then, in December of that year, a crazy Icelandic decathlete came to me with a question. "Do you want to be the best discus thrower in the world?"

My PB was only 45 meters at the time, but of course I said, yes.

"Well," the decathlete said, "If you want to be the best in the world, you must come with me in four days to California. Bruce Jenner is there, and Brian Oldfield, and Mac Wilkins."

With the help of my parents and older siblings, I was able to make the trip. We ended up staying six months, living four in an apartment and training in the same stadium as Mac, John Powell, and other top discus throwers like Art Burns, and Jim McGoldrick. Being around those guys changed my life.

When you grow up in a small country such as Iceland, it's easy to feel you don't belong on the big stage. But Mac Wilkins and John Powell never doubted they belonged, and their attitude rubbed off on me. The biggest reason I got to be a successful international coach was because of what I learned from them during my time in California.

Also on that trip, we fell into a rhythm of training I have used ever since, the one you will read about in this book. Two workouts a day for two or three days in a row, then a day of active rest, and repeat.

A few years after my first California trip, I joined a big group of Icelandic athletes, including my brother and the shot putter Hreinn Halldórsson at the University of Alabama. Hreinn was already in his thirties when he came there as a freshman. My brother--who still holds the Alabama record in the decathlon--continued to be a big influence on my training, and so was Hreinn Halldórsson, who shared with me a lot of his experience.

Another influence was Art Venegas from UCLA, who in the 1980's was already considered one of the best American coaches. We spoke during a spring break trip to California in 1985, and later Art gave me one of his yearly training plans. I combined what I learned from Art with the things my brother and Hreinn Halldórsson taught me and began to formulate my own training philosophy.

The first athlete I officially coached was Magnús Hallgrímsson, beginning in 1997, and I learned much from my experience with him. Like a lot of young coaches, I assumed what worked for me as an athlete would work for anyone. I always responded well to a high volume of training, so that is what I prescribed for Magnus. But he was a better athlete than me, with more fast-twitch muscle fibers, and I ended up training him too hard, injuring him and ruining his career. I still feel bad for my mistake, but Magnus and I are friends, and he always tells me he forgives me.

From my time with Magnus, I learned two important lessons. You must treat every athlete as an individual. And the slowest process gets the fastest result. That is the approach I used with Gerd Kanter and Daniel Ståhl, and neither of them ever had a serious injury. For this, they must thank Magnus.

All these people, and many others, contributed to my philosophy of training. I hope when you read this book, which is the story of how I prepared Daniel for the 2021 Olympics, you will take away some ideas to help you develop and refine your own methods.

2020-2021 Detailed Training Plan

In this book, I will describe the plan I devised to prepare Daniel for the Tokyo Olympics. In some ways, this plan was quite simple, as it was based on practices common among throwers since the 1980's. In other ways, it might appear complicated, as I adapted those core principles to meet the needs of a specific athlete--Daniel Ståhl--at a specific and very challenging moment in his career. I will try to explain my decisions as clearly as possible, and in doing so I will share many of the lessons I learned over the course of my long career as an athlete and coach.

I'll begin with some charts and short explanations of the various phases of Daniel's training. After that, I will go into detail about what we were attempting to accomplish in each phase and how things actually turned out. As you will see, we made many adjustments, but this is what happens when you train humans and not robots!

And remember, since this program was designed for a particular human, it would not be wise to copy it exactly for your own use. The sets, reps, percentages, and exercises you will see here were all chosen to suit Daniel's specific needs.

I hope, however, that my explanation of why we chose those sets and reps will reveal the concepts I adhered to when planning Daniel's training, concepts which may be applied to any athlete trying to achieve optimum performance.

So, here we go.

Yellow means <u>Base</u> muscle building programs - reps between 3-5 in main exercises, 10-12 reps in other exercises, sets 3-6, intensity 60-92.5%, 3-4 times/week + Eccentric

Main exercises: Back Squats, Front Squats, Sumo Deadlift, Bench Press, Incline Dumbbell Bench Press, Snatch Pulls/Box, Push Press, Shoulder Presses + some light Olympic Lifts (Specific)

Throwing 2.0kg Discus, 2.5-3.1kg Denfi Tool, total amount of throws between 40-60 a day, intensity 90-100%, 4 times/week

Red means <u>Active Rest</u> weeks - reps 5 on main exercises and 10-20 reps on other exercises, sets 5, intensity 50-60%, 2 times/week.

Main exercises: Back Squats, Bench Press + Circuit Training, and light Olympic Lifts

Throwing 2.0kg Discus, total amount of throws between 20-30 a day, intensity 80-90%, 2 times/week

Green means <u>Strength</u> or maximum capacity programs - reps between 1-5 in main exercises, 8-10 reps in other exercises, intensity 70-100%, sets 3-5, 4 times/week

Main Exercises: Power Clean, Power Snatch, Push Press, Jerk, Back Squats, Front Squats, Sumo, Bench Press, Incline Dumbbell Bench Press, Snatch Pulls/Box + Specific

Throwing 2.0kg Discus, 2.5-3.1kg Denfi Tool, total amount of throws between 30-50 a day, intensity 95-100%, 3-4 times/week + Meets

Blue means <u>Power & Speed</u> programs - reps between 1-5 in main exercises and 6-8 reps in other exercises, sets 3-5, intensity 70-90%, 3-4 times/week + Concentric.

Main Exercises: Hang Clean, Hang Snatch, Jerk, Back Squats, Front Squats, High Bench Squats, Bench Press, Sumo, Snatch Pull/Box + Specific

Throwing 2.0kg Discus, total amount of throws between 20-40 a day, intensity 95-100%, 3-4 times/week + Meets

Global Throwing

DANIEL STÅHL ANNUAL PLAN 2020-2021

DOUBLE PERIODIZATION: 2 Macrocycles, 11 Mesocycles, 3 Active Rest Cycles

MESOCYCLES:						
	Program 1	Base # 1	21 days	5-Oct-20	to	25-Oct-20
	Program 2	Base # 2	28 days	26-Oct-20	to	22-Nov-20
	Program 3	Base # 3	28 days	23-Nov-20	to	20-Dec-20
	Program 4	Active Rest # 1	14 days	21-Dec-20	to	3-Jan-21
	Program 5	Strength # 1	35 days	4-Jan-21	to	7-Feb-21
	Program 6	Active Rest # 2	7 days	8-Feb-21	to	14-Feb-21
	Program 7	Power & Speed # 1	21 days	15-Feb-21	to	7-Mar-21
	Program 8	Active Rest # 3	7 days	8-Mar-21	to	14-Mar-21
	Program 9	Base # 4	21 days	15-Mar-21	to	4-Apr-21
	Program 10	Base # 5	28 days	5-Apr-21	to	2-May-21
	Program 11	Base # 6	27 days	3-May-21	to	29-May-21
	Program 12	Strength # 2	29 days	30-May-21	to	27-Jun-21
	Program 13	Strength # 3	16 days	28-Jun-21	to	13-Jul-21
	Program 14	Power & Speed # 2	18 days	14-Jul-21	to	31-Jul-21

14 Training programs during the training year 05 October 2020 to 01 August 2021, all based on 3-5 week work cycles.

First Yellow Period - 5th October to 20th December 2020

The main goal of this first block of training was to build a base of fitness and strength to prepare Daniel for the higher intensity lifting and throwing of the later phases.

This "yellow period" was subdivided into three segments. We will examine one week from each segment to understand this phase.

5th October to 11th October (Program 1 Base 1)

Off the couch

Daniel's final competition of the 2020 season occurred on September 12. He had been resting since, so when he resumed training on October 5th, our first job was to get him up and moving before taxing his body too much. The last thing I ever wanted to do was to have one of my athletes injure themselves in training, and you risk this if you have them do too much too soon, so we always took our time getting started.

You will notice each day of this first week featured a morning session of cardio. In Daniel's case, this meant walking. When I first began training him in 2011, I started having Daniel take long walks to help him control his weight. Over the years, he came to enjoy these walks, and for a man his size, he was able to move at a very brisk pace. I know because I would sometimes accompany him, and it was not easy for me to keep up.

Even as his fitness level improved during our years together, we never graduated Daniel to running because he is a big guy with flat feet. Walking is a much safer way for him to keep in shape, so whenever you see "cardio" on his workout plan, assume it means "walking."

During the first three weeks of this early yellow phase, Daniel lifted three times per week. You will notice on all his main lifts, he did 3x5. This might seem like an unusually low number of reps for a thrower during fall training, but keep in mind that high-rep sets are designed to build muscle mass, which was not a priority with Daniel. He was already a massive guy, so there was no need to spend time making him bigger.

I have used a very different approach with Simon Pettersson. When Simon came to me, he was a skinny decathlete, so right away I had him do 24 weeks of sets with 8-12 reps to put some meat on his bones. During our entire time together, Simon always had a high-repetition phase in his plan because, unlike Daniel, he struggled to add the mass he needed to make the discus go far.

Daniel Ståhl Program 1 Base 1	05/10-25/10 2020	
SESSION 1	**SESSION 2**	
5-Oct		
Cardio 60min	**Warm up:** Bike 5-10 min	
	Olympic Warmup: Snatch Routine	
	Snatch Pull / Box	3x5x140,145,150
	Back Squats	3x5x160,180,200
	Bench Press	3x5x140,145,150
	Leg Curl	3x10-12
	Adduction	3x12-15
	ABS & STABS: Upper, lower, rotation 3 sets each, DO IT!	
	Stretch: (Back, butt, hamstring, groin, hip flexor, chest)	
6-Oct		
Cardio 60min	**Warm up:** Jog 5-10min	
	Hurdle walk or Running School: 5-10 hurdles, 5-10 ex/1-2x20-30mx5-10 ex.	
	Fitness Warmup: Tommy Routine	
	Throwing Discus: 2.0kg, 10 stand, 10 walks, 10 S&T, 10 NR, 10 R	
	Stretch: (Back, butt, hamstring, groin, hip flexor, chest)	

	7-Oct	
Cardio 60min	**Warm up:** Bike 5-10min	
	Olympic Warmup:	
	Snatch	3x3x60kg,
	Clean	3x3x100kg
	Lifting: Push Press	3x5x140,145,150
	Sumo Deadlift	3x5x200,225,250
	Press Behind Neck	3x5x80,85,90
	Reverse Fly	3x8-10
	Bent Over Row or Lat Pull	3x8-10
	ABS & STABS: Upper, lower, rotation 3 sets each, DO IT!	
	Stretch: (Back, butt, hamstring, groin, hip flexor, chest)	
	8-Oct	
Cardio 60min	**Warm up:** Jog 5-10min	
	Hurdle walk or Running School: 5-10 hurdles, 5-10 ex/1-2x20-30mx5-10 ex.	
	Fitness Warmup: Tommy Routine	
	Throwing Medicine Ball: 4-5kg, 5-10 sets, 10 reps per set	
	Stretch: (Back, butt, hamstring, groin, hip flexor, chest)	
	9-Oct	
Cardio 60min	**Warm up:** Bike 5-10min	
	Olympic Warmup: Clean Routine	
	Clean Pull / Box	3x5x160,165,170
	Front Squats	3x5x130,145,160
	Incline DB Bench Press	3x5x50,52.5,55
	Leg Curl	3x10-12
	Adduction	3x12-15
	ABS & STABS: Upper, lower, rotation 3 sets each, DO IT!	
	Stretch: (Back, butt, hamstring, groin, hip flexor, chest)	
	10-Oct	
Cardio 60min	**Warm up:** Jog 5-10min	
	Hurdle walk or Running School: 5-10 hurdles, 5-10 ex/1-2x20-30mx5-10 ex.	
	Fitness Warmup: Tommy Routine	
	Throwing Discus: 2.0kg, 10 stand, 10 walks, 10 S&T, 10 NR, 10 R	
	Stretch: (Back, butt, hamstring, groin, hip flexor, chest)	
	11-Oct	
REST	REST	

This is a lesson for coaches to keep in mind. There are certain principles of training which we are wise to follow, but to be an effective coach, you must learn to adapt your approach to fit the needs of each individual athlete. You will see many more examples of this in Daniel's training plan, including in the matter of exercise selection, which I will explain later.

The weights shown are in kilograms, and for this phase, we stayed in the 50-65% range as our goal was to get him into shape before increasing the intensity.

The little things matter

Daniel did what we call an "Olympic Warmup" before beginning his main lifts. This was a complex of exercises such as overhead squats, drop squats, and back squats all using just the 20-kilogram bar. This complex was meant as a functional flexibility exercise. Big guys like Daniel often do not love regular flexibility work such as static stretching, so I always included something like the Olympic Warmup in his routine to keep him limber.

You will also see the terms "Snatch Routine" and "Clean Routine" on his workout. These consisted of 3 sets of 3 reps with light weight (60k for snatch, 100k for cleans), where he did the full Olympic movement, again as a way of maintaining flexibility.

Another warmup we did appears on the workout plan as the "Tommy Routine." It is named after our physiotherapist, Tommy Eriksson, who was a very important member of our team. Tommy regularly checked Daniel's abdominal strength in relation to his back strength and his quad strength relative to his hamstring strength, then created rehab/prehab routines to keep everything in balance. The exact composition of these routines changed, but Tommy devised them and communicated them to Daniel, so on the workout I just put "Tommy Routine" to remind him to do it.

The Tommy Routine and the Olympic Warmup were important for keeping Daniel fit and healthy. Remember, throwing far is not just a result of being strong and technically sound--it is also about being mobile, flexible and smooth. Daniel grew up playing ice hockey, and he is remarkably agile for a guy his size, but it was important that he put in the work necessary to maintain his agility and to stay healthy. When I trained the shot putter Joachim Olsen--silver medalist at the 2004 Olympics--I had a hard time getting him to work on his flexibility, which might have been one reason why he was often injured.

The exercises I call "Abs and Stabs" also helped keep Daniel healthy. These were typical core strengthening and stability exercises, and you can see I wrote "DO IT!" next to "Abs and Stabs" on Daniel's plan. This was to remind him that even though these exercises might be boring, they were as important as anything else in our training routine.

Easy does it

During this early period, Daniel threw every other day. As with lifting, the intensity of his throwing workouts was low. Where you see "10 walks," that means he was moving through the ring at walking speed, just feeling positions before releasing the discus.

"S & T" refers to "step and turn," which for Daniel meant starting with his right foot in the middle of the circle then turning into the power position and completing the throw.

The letters "NR" mean "non-reverse," and a single letter "R" means "reverse."

During this phase, he did ten easy full throws with no reverse and ten with a reverse. As you will see, we increased the volume and intensity of throwing in later phases.

26ᵗʰ October to 1ˢᵗ November (Program 2 Base 2)

Setting the rhythm

By this point, we had switched to our typical routine of training, which consisted of a 2-2-1 pattern where we trained twice on Monday and Tuesday and once on Wednesday, then repeated the pattern on Thursday, Friday, and Saturday.

This is the same pattern I used when I was first in California with the crazy decathlete. As a coach, I have always used some version of it for one simple reason: it works!

The light day in the middle of the week allows for recovery from the preceding hard days. This gives the athletes energy to do two more hard days, which are followed by another light day and then a day of complete rest.

My athletes always enjoyed training in this pattern because they knew it gave them time to recover. And it was nice for them socially to be off from Saturday afternoon to Monday morning each week. Remember, athletes are people! They need to stay in balance physically, mentally, and socially. Yes, they must be devoted to their training, but they need time to themselves as well.

We lifted four afternoons a week during this phase. With Daniel, we paired bench press or incline dumbbell press with back or front squats on Mondays and Thursdays. On Tuesdays and Fridays, he would do sumo deadlifts or some other pull variation along with push press or another shoulder press.

Daniel Ståhl Program 2 Base 2	26/10-01/11 2020
SESSION 1	**SESSION 2**
26-Oct	
Warm up: Jog 5-10min	**Warm up:** Bike 5-10min
Hurdle walk or Running School: 5-10 hurdles, 5-10 ex/1-2x20-30mx5-10 ex.	**Olympic Warmup:** Sit Snatch 3x3x60,70,80kg
Fitness Warmup: Tommy Routine	**Lifting:** **Back Squats** 5x5x190,200,210,220,190
Throwing Discus: 2.0kg, 5 stand, 5 walks, fulls 10 NR, 15-20 R	**Incline DB Press** 5x5x53.5,56,58.5,61,53.5
Stretch: (Back, butt, hamstring, groin, hip flexor, chest)	Bent Over Row 3x8-10 or Lat Pull 3x8-10
	Leg Curl 3x10-12
	ABS & STABS: Upper, lower, rotation 3 sets each, DO IT!
27-Oct	
Warm up: Jog 5-10min	**Warm up:** Bike 5-10min
Hurdle walk or Running School: 5-10 hurdles, 5-10 ex/1-2x20-30mx5-10 ex.	**Olympic Warmup:** Clean Gymnastics
Fitness Warmup: Tommy Routine	**Lifting:** **Snatch Pull / Box** 3x5x150,155,160
Throwing Discus: 2.0kg, 10 stand, 10 walks, 10 S&T, 10 NR, 10 R	**Push Press** 4x5x150,155,160,150
Stretch: (Back, butt, hamstring, groin, hip flexor, chest)	Reverse Fly 3x8-10
	Adduction 3x12-15
	ABS & STABS: Upper, lower, rotation 3 sets each, DO IT!
28-Oct	
Warm up: Jog 5-10min	**REST**
Hurdle walk or Running School: 5-10 hurdles, 5-10 ex/1-2x20-30mx5-10 ex.	
Gymnastics, medicine ball, fitness	
Rehab, Prehab	
Extra Stretch	
Cardio	

29-Oct	
Warm up: Jog 5-10min	**Warm up:** Bike 5-10min
Hurdle walk or Running School: 5-10 hurdles, 5-10 ex/1-2x20-30mx5-10 ex.	**Olympic Warmup:** Sit Clean　　　　　3x3x100,110,120kg
Fitness Warmup: Tommy Routine	**Lifting:** **Bench Press** 　　　　5x5x140,145,150,155,140
Throwing Denfi 2.5kg-3.1kg: 30-40 throws NR	**Front Squats** 　　　　5x5x135,145,155,145,135
Stretch: (Back, butt, hamstring, groin, hip flexor, chest)	Bent Over Row　　　3x8-10 or Lat Pull　　　　　　3x8-10
	Leg Curl　　　　　　3x10-12
	ABS & STABS: Upper, lower, rotation 3 sets each, DO IT!
30-Oct	
Warm up: Jog 5-10min	**Warm up:** Bike 5-10min
Hurdle walk or Running School: 5-10 hurdles, 5-10 ex/1-2x20-30mx5-10 ex.	**Olympic Warmup:** Snatch Gymnastics
Fitness Warmup: Tommy Routine	**Lifting:** **Sumo Deadlift**　　4x5x240,250,260,270
Throwing Discus: 2.0kg, 10 stand, 10 walks, 10 S&T, 10 NR, 10 R	**Press Behind Neck/Sitting**　3x5x90,92.5,95
Stretch: (Back, butt, hamstring, groin, hip flexor, chest)	Reverse Fly　　　　　　3x8-10
	Adduction　　　　　　　3x12-15
	ABS & STABS: Upper, lower, rotation 3 sets each, DO IT!
31-Oct	
Warm up: Jog 5-10min	**REST**
Hurdle walk or Running School: 5-10 hurdles, 5-10 ex/1-2x20-30mx5-10 ex.	
Gymnastics, medicine ball, fitness	
Rehab, Prehab	
Extra Stretch	
Cardio	
1-Nov	
REST	REST

  I did not use an upper/lower split with my athletes because it is too much to put all the lower body lifts on one day. Whenever I tried an upper/lower split over the years, my athletes accused me of trying to kill them. Even doing bench and overhead presses on the same day can be too much. I know the upper/lower split is common in America, and though much of what I do is influenced by my experiences training and competing there and by my knowledge of the systems used by coaches such as Art Venegas and Don Babbitt, on this I took a different path.

I believe a thrower needs to be able to throw far during every phase of training. Are they going to be able to throw as far in a high-volume phase as they do in a peaking phase? No. If we do our job properly, they will always have the highest energy level, the greatest power output, the best rhythm, and therefore the farthest throws during the final phase of our training plan.

But the 2-2-1 training setup and a careful approach to weightlifting allowed my athletes to throw pretty well during all phases, which is important. A thrower must constantly work to develop and maintain a rhythm and "feel" for the throw, and they cannot do this if they are totally exhausted from lifting weights.

The Big Four

The main lifts we used with Daniel were back squats, bench presses, sumo deadlifts and push presses. After the first three weeks of the program, he almost always did two of those lifts per session, usually either squats paired with bench presses or deadlifts paired with push presses. He was meant to do each of the main lifts twice per week, but during the most strenuous periods of training he would often do the main exercise (back squats, for example) once and a variation of that exercise (front squats, for example) once.

Our plan for the week of 26th October illustrates this. You see on Monday we paired back squat with incline dumbbell press, then on Thursday bench press with front squat. On Tuesday he did snatch pull and push press, then switched to sumo deadlift and seated press-behind-the-neck on Friday. Using these alternate exercises was part of our effort to keep him strong without killing him and making it impossible for him to function in the ring.

Mr. Sumo?

Also, speaking of exercise selection, I got a reputation over the years as a "deadlift guy." This was because of lifting videos Daniel posted to social media which showed him using the sumo-style deadlift to move a lot of weight. People loved those videos, but the reputation I got is not necessarily accurate. I believe pulling exercises are important, but there are many different kinds of pulls—deadlifts, clean pulls, snatch pulls, full cleans, full snatches—that can be used, and it is vital to figure out which exercises best suit each athlete.

So, why did we choose sumo deadlifts as a main lift for Daniel instead of cleans or snatches?

Our reliance on the power lifts (back squat, bench press, sumo deadlift) for Daniel was not because I am against using Olympic lifts to train throwers. If you looked at YouTube during Gerd Kanter's prime years, you probably saw videos of him performing heavy reps on the Olympic lifts. This worked well for Gerd, but Daniel's physical makeup is very different. Gerd had the ability to sustain a high level of intensity throughout a training session. During one practice, he surpassed 70 meters on 40 consecutive throws! Another time, he took 140 throws in one session, and his last several attempts were over 70 meters! Fanny Roos is like that, too, and so is Simon Pettersson. In one session, when we were throwing the Denfi tool into a net, Simon took 137 throws in 75 minutes. A workout like that might kill Daniel.

I have seen Daniel throw 70 meters multiple times in one session, but he needed to sit down and gather himself after every couple of attempts. This was not because he is lazy. He is simply a huge guy, and it takes a lot out of him to move his big body explosively.

In selecting the lifts for Daniel's program, we took his physical qualities into account. For him, throwing the discus was his main explosive exercise, so the Olympic lifts were mostly unnecessary and potentially harmful because they might exhaust him to the point where he would lose the feeling in his throws.

And even with throwers like Gerd, Simon, and Fanny, who possessed a greater work capacity than Daniel, I did not train them like Olympic weightlifters. Think of this. An Olympic weightlifter might, as the main portion of their workout, perform multiple sets of one rep of full snatches at 90-100% intensity. This is a fantastic way to build explosive power.

But, prior to their workout, an Olympic lifter would not have performed fifty explosive movements in the discus ring. When a thrower enters the weight room, though, they may have just come from an intense throwing practice, or they may have a throwing workout later that day or the next morning. A coach must consider how the combination of throwing and lifting is going to affect each athlete and make sure the athlete is able to recover from every session.

As I said, I am not against using the Olympic lifts in the training of throwers. Simon and Fanny did them often in their training. But a coach must find ways to effectively integrate these explosive movements into the athletes' training plans rather than just borrowing a program from a weightlifter and putting their thrower's name on it.

For Daniel, deadlifts worked better than cleans or snatches as a main lift because they were easier on his body and allowed him to get the most out of his throwing sessions even as we were making him stronger.

Another reason we chose sumo deadlifts for Daniel is because he enjoyed them and truly believed they made him throw farther. Over time, we even developed the habit of having him perform sumo deadlifts two days before a competition.

At a Diamond League final a few years ago, he was scheduled to compete on a Saturday, which meant we would normally do sumo deadlifts on Thursday and rest on Friday. But his knee felt sore that Wednesday, so we did not do the Thursday sumo deadlifts, and he threw badly at the Saturday competition. He told me afterward he had lost his feeling for the throw. When we flew home, we went straight from the airport to the weight room so he could get in his sumo deadlifts before his next competition. There, he ended up throwing very well.

I know it is fine for an athlete to rest for three or four days before a competition. In fact, it is sometimes the best thing to do physically if they have been competing and traveling a lot. But you must have the athlete with you when you decide these things, and if they believe doing sumo deadlift two days before competing is essential, then you must take that into account.

So, am I a "deadlift guy"? With Daniel, yes, because he believed in it, and it worked for him.

And we did use a bit of Olympic lifting with Daniel. As I said, we often used snatch pulls from knee-high blocks as his alternative exercise for deadlifts. Pulling from knee height was best for him because it eliminated much of the stress on his body. Also, as you saw earlier, we used light Olympic lifts as a warmup to help him maintain his mobility and avoid becoming too much like a bulldozer.

Speaking of mobility, you will see in this training week I used the terms "sit snatch" and "sit clean" as part of Daniel's "Olympic Warmup." This was my way of telling him to do the full movement--in other words, to take each snatch or clean into a full squat.

You will also see the terms "snatch gymnastics" and "clean gymnastics," which is just another way of describing the complex of movements with the bare bar which I explained earlier.

The 1980's, modified

The sets and reps from this point on in the yellow phase were a variation on the classic 5x5 program from the 1980s. The original 5x5 from the '80s would be all five sets at 80%, but we never did this with Daniel. Instead, we raised and lowered the percentage throughout the five sets. For example, we might do the first set of five at 70%, the second set at 75%, the third set at 80%, then back to 75% for the fourth set and finish with a set at 70%. At the end of the yellow phase, we sometimes switched to 5x3, and then we could go up to 90%, but again only for one of the five sets.

I took this approach because, as I've explained, even in this base-strength phase, I never wanted to wear Daniel out in the weight room to the detriment of his throwing. Performing one "heavy" set during each 5x5 session got Daniel strong while conserving energy for the ring. Over the course of the yellow phase, the heavy set got slightly heavier each week. Daniel would barely feel the difference, and throughout this phase he got stronger without hurting himself or feeling too sore to throw.

As I mentioned, the yellow phase was divided into blocks of approximately four weeks. During the first block, most work is done in the 60-70% percent range. This changed to 70-80% in the second block and 75-85% or even 90% in the final block. The October 26th sample week is the beginning of the second block.

These percentages applied only to the main lifts we used with Daniel: back squat, bench press, sumo deadlift, and push press. When we did the alternative lifts (snatch pull, front squat, behind-the-neck-press, dumbbell bench press), we did not regularly increase the weight from week to week. Those lifts were strictly for volume.

A tool of the trade

A typical throwing session for Daniel during this period began with a few dry throws to get warmed up, followed by 5 stands, 5 walking throws with static positions, 5-10 non-reverse fulls, and 15-20 fulls with reverse. He also, as you can see, began training with the 3-kilogram Denfi tool.

When we threw the discus tool, we threw only the tool and did not take reps with the normal implement. The focus when we used the tool was to take hard, technically sound throws. The Denfi device allowed Daniel to perform technically solid reps with a heavier load than the two-kilo discus. This developed specific strength without messing up his form. We usually threw the tool into a net. Occasionally, at training camps, we threw it out into the field, but throwing it into a net lets you forget about how far it is going and keeps the focus on technique. This was our only "throwing strength" exercise. We did nothing in the weight room to mimic throwing movements. Some people might be surprised to hear this, but throwers hate exercises like turns with a lifting bar on their back and mimicking throwing movements with a medicine ball. These are a waste of time if you are able to use the throwing tool instead.

We discovered with Gerd Kanter that his technique was actually better with the tool than with the discus. This was a dream scenario for a coach because it allowed us to reinforce sound positions while at the same time building strength. It did not always work this way, though. Another athlete I trained, Nick Percy, was so strong he could throw the tool far with poor technique, so we dropped it from his training because we never wanted to build bad habits.

When we first introduced the tool into his training each year, Daniel usually could not execute more than 25 throws with it, but we eventually got to the point where he could perform 40 or even 50 full, non-reverse throws in a single session.

During this period, Daniel's throwing practices were mostly what I call "technical" sessions. On these days, we would work up to fulls at about 90% effort. In Daniel's case, these would be throws in the 65-meter range. The focus was on rhythm and technique. Sometimes we would do a drill between each throw. In total, he would perform around 50 throws on technical days, but the number could vary depending on his energy level. I always had a number in mind going into each session of how many total throws I wanted the athlete to take, but there was improvisation within each session as well. On certain days, for example, we'd end up doing more non-reverse throws than usual. It depended on how things were going during the session and what we decided to focus on.

Recovery time

Wednesdays and Saturdays were, as I said, recovery days in this program, and I gave the athletes input regarding the activities they would do on these days. There were many possibilities, including total rest if they were feeling worn out. Sometimes they chose fitness or flexibility exercises such as running school, gymnastics, or hurdle walking. Other times, they focused on prehab or rehab work. They could also choose a fun activity like basketball, or Daniel would sometimes take his 90-minute walk.

23rd November to 29th November (Program 3 Base 3)

Finding a balance

Earlier, I described the 2-2-1, 2-2-1 pattern we used for most of our training weeks. You will notice during this week we used a slightly different pattern.

Day one was normal, with throwing in the morning and then lifting in the afternoon, but on day two, Daniel did only one session. This was to allow him time to travel to Stockholm.

Daniel grew up near Stockholm, and his parents and sister still live there. It was, for several years, hard for him to get used to living most of the time in Växjö where our training was based, because he missed his family and friends. Eventually, we figured out a way to keep him feeling balanced socially and mentally by having him return home for a week or two occasionally.

We usually worked this out when going over our training plan prior to each season. He loved spending time at home and lifting with his friends at his local gym, the Stockholm Athletic Club, which is one of those weight rooms that makes you feel like it is still the 1970s. Usually, after a week of training at home, Daniel was excited to return to Växjö and resume working with the group and with me.

Obviously, it was important for me to be present for most of Daniel's training sessions, but it was also important for him to feel happy, and the trips home made him very happy.

And I learned while coaching Gerd Kanter that not being together all the time can make the sessions you do have together more productive. The whole time I was his coach, Gerd lived in Estonia, and I lived in either Sweden or Denmark. One of us had to travel for us to train together in person, and when we were together, we always got a tremendous amount of work done. There was a kind of magic from not being together every single day. Gerd was always extremely excited for our "training camps" and always got better from them.

Daniel Ståhl Program 3 Base 3	23/11-20/12 2020
SESSION 1	**SESSION 2**
23-Nov	
Warm up: Jog 5-10min	**Warm up:** Bike 5-10min
Hurdle walk or Running School: 5-10 hurdles, 5-10 ex/1-2x20-30mx5-10 ex.	**Olympic Warmup:** Sit Snatch 3x3x70,80,90kg
Fitness Warmup: Tommy Routine	**Lifting: Back Squats** 5x5x200,210,220,230,200
Throwing Discus: 2.0kg, 5 stand, 5 walks, fulls 10 NR, 15-20 R	**Incline Dumbbell Press** 5x5x56,58.5,61,58.5,56
Stretch: (Back, butt, hamstring, groin, hip flexor, chest)	Bent Over Row or Lat Pull 3x8-10
	Leg Curl 3x10-12
	ABS & STABS: Upper, lower, rotation 3 sets each, DO IT!

24-Nov	
REST (Rest till Stockholm)	**Warm up:** Bike 5-10min
	Olympic Warmup: Clean Gymnastics
	Lifting: **Snatch Pull / Box** **3x5x160,165,170**
	Push Press **4x5x155,160,165,155**
	Reverse Fly 3x8-10
	Adduction 3x12-15
	ABS & STABS: Upper, lower, rotation 3 sets each, DO IT!
25-Nov	
Cardio 60-90min	**Warm up:** Jog 5-10min
	Hurdle walk or Running School: 5-10 hurdles, 5-10 ex/1-2x20-30mx5-10 ex.
	Fitness Warmup: Tommy Routine
	Throwing Denfi 2.5kg-3.1kg: 30-40 throws NR
	Stretch: (Back, butt, hamstring, groin, hip flexor, chest)
26-Nov	
Cardio 60-90min	**Warm up:** Bike 5-10min
	Olympic Warmup: Sit Clean 3x3x110,120,130kg
	Lifting: **Bench Press** **5x5x150,155,160,165,150**
	Front Squats **3x5x145,155,165**
	Bent Over Row 3x8-10 or Lat Pull 3x8-10
	Leg Curl 3x10-12
	ABS & STABS: Upper, lower, rotation 3 sets each, DO IT!
27-Nov	
Cardio 60-90min	**Warm up:** Jog 5-10min
	Hurdle walk or Running School: 5-10 hurdles, 5-10 ex/1-2x20-30mx5-10 ex.
	Fitness Warmup: Tommy Routine
	Throwing Discus: 2.0kg, 10 stand, 10 walks, 10 S&T, 10 NR, 10 R
	Stretch: (Back, butt, hamstring, groin, hip flexor, chest)

28-Nov	
Warm up: Bike 5-10min	**Cardio** 60-90min
Olympic Warmup: Snatch Gymnastics	
Lifting:	
Sumo Deadlift 4x5x250,260,270,280	
Press Behind Neck/Seated 3x5x90,95,100	
Reverse Fly 3x8-10	
Adduction 3x12-15	
ABS & STABS: Upper, lower, rotation 3 sets each, DO IT!	
29-Nov	
REST	**REST**

Daniel's situation was similar. He felt refreshed when he spent a week in Stockholm, which kept him happy and let us get the most out of our time together in Växjö.

You can see he completed his four lifting sessions during this week and was using heavier weights than during the October 26th week, which we examined earlier. During that week, he did 5x5 back squats, starting with a set at 190 kilos and working up to a heavy set at 220 kilos. During the week of November 23rd, he was still doing 5x5, but the weight had increased so that he opened with a set at 200 kilos and worked up to a heavy set at 230 kilos.

In bench press, he did 5x5 starting with a set of 140 kilos and working up to 155 kilos in October, and by late November was doing his first set of five with 150 kilos and working up to 165 kilos.

He was also, by late November, using five kilos more for each set of push press than he had in October.

This was typical of the simple approach we used. We generally stuck with the same main lifts, gradually changing the sets, reps, and intensity.

Remember, our goal was always to get stronger without risking injury and without making it impossible for Daniel to move in the ring.

Variety is the spice...

That said, I made little changes in Daniel's program more often than with any of my other throwers due to his personality. When it came to training, Gerd Kanter was a machine. For the first eight years I coached him, he never asked a single question about his program other than, "What would you like me to do today?"

Daniel was different, and this made training him both more interesting and more challenging. For example, he might come to me four weeks into the yellow phase and ask, "How long are we going to do five-by-five?"

I would remind him we had only been on five-by-five for four weeks and that he usually loved five-by-five, but I would also adjust the sets and reps if that is what he preferred.

Or he might ask, "How long are we going to do push press?"

I might tell him I was planning for him to do push press for several more weeks, but if he said he was tired of it, I would take it out of his routine.

Then, two weeks later, he might ask when he would be allowed to do push press again.

He did not do this to drive me crazy. It is just the way he is. Daniel gets bored much more easily than Gerd, Simon, or Fanny, and to help him achieve his best results, I had to take this into account.

During December of 2020, at the end of the yellow phase, I received a call from Daniel when he was training in Stockholm. "Hey," he asked, "can I do some heavy deadlifts today?" It turns out some of his friends were coming to the weight room, and he wanted to show off a bit.

I gave him permission. Why? Because it made him feel good to show his friends how strong he had gotten.

Making these small concessions while staying within the boundaries of the overall plan helped me keep him focused and excited about training.

The best ones are different

I saw a video during the spring of 2021 where Joe Kovacs squatted 870 pounds for a set of four reps. At that stage of his career, did Joe Kovacs really need to train with such heavy weight? Strictly speaking, no. It was probably not worth the risk of injury.

But remember, Joe is a unique person and his coach--Ashley Kovacs--is also his wife, so she understands him probably better even than a normal coach could. Maybe making those reps with a huge weight helped give him confidence in his battles with Ryan Crouser. Maybe it was Joe's way of sending Crouser a message that he was not ready to concede the World title he won in 2019. Only Joe and Ashley know for sure, but when I saw this video, it reminded me of Daniel.

Guys like Joe Kovacs and Daniel Ståhl are not like you and me. They are World champions and face a lot of pressure to stay on top in their event. If doing heavy sumo deadlifts in a basement gym in Stockholm or taking reps with 870 pounds in a squat rack in Columbus, Ohio, gives them the confidence they need to take on the world's best, then so be it.

Strong man

One slight change we made during this period, which you may notice, is the sets on front squats went from 5x5 in October to 3x5 in November. I did this because I could see that doing 5x5 on back squats (which for Daniel, was his main leg-strengthening lift) wore him out to the point where doing another 5x5 on front squats in the same week was not a good idea. As you can see, dropping to 3x5 allowed him to increase the weight he used by 10 kilos--the same increase as with back squats and bench presses--over the course of a month, so we were able to make him stronger in a way which did not wreck him.

During this week, when he was in Stockholm, we dropped one throwing session in order to give him time to travel, but you will see that the three sessions he took were similar to the sessions we had been doing since October. With the discus, he was still feeling out positions with a lot of stands, walking throws, step and turns, and non-reverse fulls. With the Denfi tool, he did between 30 and 40 non-reverse fulls.

His throwing sessions would get a bit more focused and intense during the next training period.

By the end of the yellow phase, if everything happens as planned, a thrower goes from the sofa to world-class shape, and this is how it worked for Daniel during the fall and winter of 2020-2021.

Daniel's base strength was very good at the end of the yellow period.

Here were some of his lifting numbers. As usual, they are in kilograms.

Back Squat 1x300 easy
Sumo Deadlift 3x330 easy
Bench Press 1x200
Push Press 3x180 easy

I could tell Daniel was tired when this yellow phase ended in December, so I gave him two weeks of active rest before embarking on the first green phase. In the charts above, the active rest phases appear in red.

Red Period - 21st December 2020 to 3rd January 2021

On the year plan you will see "red" weeks between some of the yellow, green, and blue phases. These are weeks of active rest which allowed Daniel to recover from the stress of heavy lifting and throwing.

During red weeks, Daniel would train once a day on anywhere from three to five days. The intensity in lifting dropped to 60-70%, and he usually did only bench and squats with maybe some very light Olympic lifting. During a red week, he would generally do two lifting sessions with at least 72 hours between them.

Throwing would consist of two sessions of 20-30 full throws at low intensity.

Red weeks also included two cardio sessions of approximately 60 minutes, which for Daniel would be walking or pedaling a stationary bike.

First Green Period - 4th January to 7th February 2021

1st February to 7th February 2021 (Program 5 Strength 1)

And now, the hard part

This was the phase during which we reached the highest intensity levels in the weight room with sets in the 90+ percent range while at the same time demanding more of Daniel in his throwing sessions. This put a lot of stress on his body, so we had to be careful to balance his weight training with his throwing to avoid pushing him into exhaustion and possible injury.

One way we managed this was by maintaining the 2-2-1 pattern in his training. Having an active rest day after every two hard days of training and also having one day of total rest each week gave Daniel a chance to recover from the high intensity work this phase required.

After building a solid base of strength in the yellow period, Daniel was now ready to move some heavy kilos, especially as we dropped the number of sets and reps in his main lifts. As you saw earlier, during the week of November 23rd, Daniel did 5x5 in back squats with 200, 210, 220, 230, and 200 kilos. In this example from the green phase, he lifted 3x3 with 250, 270, and 290 kilos. That's a lot of weight, but as in the yellow phase, we had Daniel work up to one "heavy" set each session, which enabled him to build strength without emptying his tank.

You'll notice that we reduced the sets and reps on all his main lifts except seated press-behind-the-neck. This exercise was an exception because it was not one in which we ever wanted to approach maximal weight. It was important to keep Daniel's shoulders strong and healthy and to balance out his bench press, but the seated pressing position is not ideal for safely attempting heavy reps, so we stayed with 3x5.

Daniel Ståhl Program 5 Strength 1	01/02-07/02 2021
SESSION 1	SESSION 2
1-Feb	
Warm up: Jog 5-10min	**Warm up:** Bike 5-10min
Hurdle walk or Running School: 5-10 hurdles, 5-10 ex/1-2x20-30mx5-10 ex.	**Olympic Warmup:** Sit Snatch 3,2,1x80,90,100kg
Fitness Warmup: Tommy Routine	**Lifting:** **Back Squats** 3x3x250,270,290
Throwing Discus: 2.0kg, 5 stands, 5 walks, 5 fulls NR, 10-15 fulls R 95-100%	**Incline Dumbbell Press** 3x5x58.5,61,63.5
Stretch: (Back, butt, hamstring, groin, hip flexor, chest)	Bent Over Row or Lat Pull 3x8-10
	Leg Curl 3x10-12
Slam session: 6 hard throws	**ABS & STABS:** Upper, lower, rotation 3 sets each, DO IT!
2-Feb	
Warm up: Jog 5-10min	**Warm up:** Bike 5-10min
Hurdle walk or Running School: 5-10 hurdles, 5-10 ex/1-2x20-30mx5-10 ex.	**Olympic Warmup:** Clean Gymnastics
Fitness Warmup: Tommy Routine	**Lifting:** **Snatch Pull / Box** 5,4,3x170,175,180
Throwing Discus: 2.0kg, 30-40 fulls R, put as many as you can in control on 65m, 90%	**Push Press** 3x2x180,185,190
Stretch: (Back, butt, hamstring, groin, hip flexor, chest)	Reverse Fly 3x8-10
	Adduction 3x12-15
	ABS & STABS: Upper, lower, rotation 3 sets each, DO IT!
3-Feb	
Warm up: Jog 5-10min	**REST**
Hurdle walk or Running School: 5-10 hurdles, 5-10 ex/1-2x20-30mx5-10 ex.	
Gymnastics, medicine ball, fitness	
Rehab, Prehab	
Extra Stretch	
Cardio	

4-Feb	
Warm up: Jog 5-10min	**Olympic Warmup:** Sit Clean 3,2,1x120,130,140kg
Hurdle walk or Running School: 5-10 hurdles, 5-10 ex/1-2x20-30mx5-10 ex.	**Lifting:** **Bench Press**　　　3x3x180,190,200
Fitness Warmup: Tommy Routine	**Front Squats**　　5,4,3x160,170,180
Throwing Discus: 2.0kg, 5 stands, 5 walks, 10 fulls NR, 15-20 fulls R 90%	Bent Over Row　　3x8-10　or Lat Pull　　　　　3x8-10
Stretch: (Back, butt, hamstring, groin, hip flexor, chest)	Leg Curl　　　　　3x10-12
	ABS & STABS: Upper, lower, rotation 3 sets each, DO IT!
5-Feb	
Warm up: Jog 5-10min	**Warm up:** Bike 5-10min
Hurdle walk or Running School: 5-10 hurdles, 5-10 ex/1-2x20-30mx5-10 ex.	**Olympic Warmup:** Snatch Gymnastics
Fitness Warmup: Tommy Routine	**Lifting:** **Sumo Deadlift**　　3x2x300,310,320
Throwing Denfi 2.8kg-3.1kg: 30-40 throws NR 100%	**Press Behind Neck/Seated** 　　　　　　　　　3x5x100,105,110
Stretch: (Back, butt, hamstring, groin, hip flexor, chest)	Reverse Fly　　　3x8-10
	Adduction　　　　3x12-15
	ABS & STABS: Upper, lower, rotation 3 sets each, DO IT!
6-Feb	
Warm up: Jog 5-10min	**REST**
Hurdle walk or Running School: 5-10 hurdles, 5-10 ex/1-2x20-30mx5-10 ex.	
Gymnastics, medicine ball, fitness	
Rehab, Prehab	
Extra Stretch	
Cardio	
7-Feb	
REST	**REST**

As you can also see from the sample week, Daniel's main exercises stayed the same from the yellow to the green phase. I do not believe in making changes just to change, and I often reminded myself to stick with what worked. This probably set me apart from other coaches, but I took great care to select particular exercises which suited each individual athlete, and changing the sets, reps, and intensity from phase to phase usually provided enough variety.

Time to slam

As I said, we also raised the intensity in the throwing ring during this phase, and you can see an example in his session on February 1st. As in the yellow phase, Daniel began with stands, walking throws, and non-reverse fulls, but this time he was meant to go much harder on his full-throws-with-reverse. Those 10-15 fulls would include 6 at competition effort. I called these practices "slam sessions," and they were a good indicator of how Daniel's training was going. They were also fun and provided a nice bit of motivation during the long winter. Also, throwing far, even if your body is worn out from heavy training, builds confidence. Remember, one of the biggest challenges a thrower faces at this level is making it through qualification at major championships. The more times a male discus thrower can reach 65 meters or better--including in a slam session indoors during a heavy training phase--the more likely it is that he will throw far when it counts the most.

We worked on this also during his second throwing session of the week. The second session was meant to be not as intense as the slam session, but still a challenging workout with many full throws. The focus in sessions like this was consistency, and ideally, Daniel would drop throw after throw on the 65-meter line.

The third session this week was more of a technical session, starting with stands and walks and leading up to non-reverse and reverse fulls at less than 100% effort.

Our final throwing session was with the Denfi tool, and it was also very intense: non-reverse full throws only, at 100% effort.

I tried to arrange these throwing sessions in a way to help Daniel recover. The slam session came after a full day of rest, so he would have plenty of energy. The Denfi session, which also could be exhausting, came at the end of the week, so he would have the weekend to rest.

Stronger still

As you will see, the second green phase, which would take place in June when Daniel was traveling and competing often, would be trickier to manage than this first one. Covid made this even more complicated than usual, and there would be times during the 2021 season when I was worried Daniel might break down physically. We will get to that later. For now, I will say I was mostly happy with how this first green phase worked out. By the end of it, Daniel was extremely strong. Here are some of his lifts:

Back Squat 1x300-320 (Estimated max 320)
Sumo Deadlift 3x330 (Estimated max 400)
Push Press 2x190 (Estimated max 205)
Bench Press 3x200 (Estimated max 215)

He also threw many times between 68-70 meters in our indoor facility. His technique and feeling, though, were still not as I wanted. And at times, his enthusiasm was a bit low, mainly because he did not love throwing indoors.

First Blue Period – 15th February to 7th March 2021

15th February to 21st February (Program 7 Power & Speed 1)

Into the blue

The blue phase in our program was the peaking phase. Simply put, we would drop the volume and intensity of our training so Daniel could devote more energy to throwing far.

This particular blue phase was originally meant to last four weeks and end with us competing at the European Throwing Cup in Leiria, Portugal, on March 13th and 14th. Daniel's performance there would give me a chance to see how effective our winter training had been.

We loved throwing in Leiria because of the atmosphere, which is funny because the facilities are lousy. The throwing field is just a grass patch by a highway which doesn't drain very well when it rains--and it always rains. The weight room is old with equipment from ancient times. But Paulo Reis--the coach of Auriol Dongmo--always hosted the Throwing Cup, and he made everyone feel welcome. A lot of people from the throwing community showed up every year, and it was fun to see them and to hang out together for a few days.

Unfortunately, the 2021 Throwing Cup was canceled because of Covid, so I decided to test Daniel's fitness by having him attempt to break the unofficial indoor world discus record at our hall in Växjö on March 7th.

You can see, based on the sample week from this period, that we made a slight change to our usual 2-2-1, 2-2-1 routine. Daniel threw in the morning and lifted in the afternoon on Monday, Tuesday, Thursday, and Friday and had one easy session of fitness/mobility on Wednesday morning. The difference this week was that he did not have a morning session on Saturday and instead got two full days of rest to finish the week. This was in keeping with our goal of letting him have lots of energy for our throwing sessions.

Keeping the big guy happy

We did not change the main lifts during this blue phase. I usually respected Daniel's wishes on this. Sometimes, he just wanted to do bench press, back squat, push press, and sumo deadlift during a peaking phase because those were the lifts he enjoyed the most. Sometimes he liked having more variety, so we kept front squats and the other alternative lifts. I always felt him out because I wanted him to be happy and confident and ready to throw far during our blue phases.

Daniel Ståhl Prog 7 Power & Speed #1		15/02-07/03 2021	
SESSION 1		**SESSION 2**	
15-Feb			
Warm up: Jog 5-10min		**Warm up:** Bike 5-10min	
Hurdle walk or Running School: 5-10 hurdles, 5-10 ex/1-2x20-30mx5-10 ex.		**Olympic Warmup:** Sit Snatch	3x1x100+
Fitness Warmup: Tommy Routine		**Lifting:** Back Squats	5,4,3x225,240,255
Throwing Discus: 2.0kg, 5 walks NR, 5 static fulls NR, 5 fulls NR, 10-15 fulls R 95-100%		**Bench Press**	3x5x150,160,170
		Bent Over Row Lat Pull	3x8-10 or 3x8-10
Stretch: (Back, butt, hamstring, groin, hip flexor, chest)		Leg Curl	3x10-12
Good technique, control, no fouls, slam on 6 throws		**ABS & STABS:** Upper, lower, rotation 3 sets each, DO IT!	

16-Feb	
Warm up: Jog 5-10min	**Warm up:** Bike 5-10min
Hurdle walk or Running School: 5-10 hurdles, 5-10 ex/1-2x20-30mx5-10 ex.	**Olympic Warmup:** Clean Gymnastics
Fitness Warmup: Tommy Routine	**Lifting:** Snatch Pull / Box 3x5x170,175,180
Throwing Discus + Drills: 2.0kg, Drills + 5 fulls NR, 15 fulls R submax, 95%	Push Press 5,4,3x150,160,170
	Reverse Fly 3x8-10
Stretch: (Back, butt, hamstring, groin, hip flexor, chest)	Adduction 3x12-15
Drills, video, 20 controlled throws of 65m with good tech.	**ABS & STABS:** Upper, lower, rotation 3 sets each, DO IT!

17-Feb	
Warm up: Jog 5-10min	**REST**
Hurdle walk or Running School: 5-10 hurdles, 5-10 ex/1-2x20-30mx5-10 ex.	
Gymnastics, medicine ball, fitness	
Rehab, Prehab	
Extra Stretch	
Cardio	

18-Feb	
Warm up: Jog 5-10min	**Warm up:** Bike 5-10min
Hurdle walk or Running School: 5-10 hurdles, 5-10 ex/1-2x20-30mx5-10 ex.	**Olympic Warmup:** Sit Clean 3x1x140+
Fitness Warmup: Tommy Routine	**Lifting:** Incline DB Bench 5,4,3x63.5,66,68.5-71
Throwing Discus: 2.0kg, 5 walks NR, 5 static fulls NR, 5 fulls NR, 10-15 fulls R 95-100%	Front Squats 3x5x150,155,160
	Bent Over Row 3x8-10 or Lat Pull 3x8-10
Stretch: (Back, butt, hamstring, groin, hip flexor, chest)	Leg Curl 3x10-12
Good technique, control, no fouls, stability. No slam, but control on 6 throws	**ABS & STABS:** Upper, lower, rotation 3 sets each, DO IT!

19-Feb	
Warm up: Jog 5-10min	**Warm up:** Bike 5-10min
Hurdle walk or Running School: 5-10 hurdles, 5-10 ex/1-2x20-30mx5-10 ex.	**Olympic Warmup:** Snatch Gymnastics
Fitness Warmup: Tommy Routine	**Lifting:** **Sumo Deadlift** 5,4,3x260,280,300
Throwing Discus + Drills: 2.0kg, Drills + 5 fulls NR, 15 fulls R submax, 95%	**Press Behind Neck/Sitting** 3x5x100,105,110
	Reverse Fly 3x8-10
Stretch: (Back, butt, hamstring, groin, hip flexor, chest)	Adduction 3x12-15
Drills, video, 20 controlled throws of 65m, good technique	**ABS & STABS:** Upper, lower, rotation 3 sets each, DO IT!
20-Feb	
REST	REST
21-Feb	
REST	REST

Throughout my career, I spent a tremendous amount of time writing and rewriting workout plans because I always wanted to get them just right for each individual athlete. It took me at least two or three hours to write a four-week block of training for each of my throwers. Much of that time was spent going back over plans we used in previous years. I looked to see what worked and did not work in the past, and then tried to apply those lessons as we moved forward.

I never gave one of my athletes a plan until I was completely satisfied with it, but even then, I sometimes ended up having to make revisions.

With Gerd, once I sent him the workout, I had to make very few adjustments. He was comfortable letting me make all the decisions. Fanny and Simon were like that as well. Sometimes, I had to modify the way we did a lift to keep them healthy. Simon, for example, because he is so tall, might do snatch pulls from blocks instead of the floor if his back felt tight. But athletes like Gerd, Simon, and Fanny are mostly content to just follow the plan.

The person I spent the most time writing plans for in my career was Joachim Olsen. It would take us something like nine hours of discussing and revising to come up with each four-to-six-week cycle. Then, a week into the program, he would want to change it.

Daniel was somewhere in between Joachim and Gerd. He liked for me to write the plan, and when I gave it to him, he always said, "Great plan, man!" Then, a couple of weeks later, he might get frustrated with his progress on bench presses and ask to switch to dumbbell bench presses for a while.

But this is the art of coaching. Daniel, Joachim, and Gerd were all great throwers, but also humans, and not all humans are the same. It was up to me to adjust my approach to get the best out of each of them.

Let me return now to explain the sample week from this blue period.

Same lifts, only faster

You can see that even though we had Daniel do the same lifts, we significantly lowered the intensity of his main exercises.

During the week of February 1st, for example, Daniel did 3x3 on back squats with 250, 270, and 290 kilos. Then, two weeks later, as we began the blue phase, he did 5,4,3 on back squats with much lighter weights: 225, 240, and 255 kilos.

It was the same in bench press, push press, front squats, and sumo deadlift. We dropped the intensity and emphasized moving the weight with speed. This gave him a chance to recover from the hard training of the yellow and green phases and left energy in the tank which he could use in the ring.

You may notice, however, that we did not drop the intensity in three of the alternative lifts. During the week of February 1st, Daniel did 5,4,3 on snatch pulls with 170, 175, and 180 kilos. In the sample week provided from this blue phase, you can see that Daniel did 3x5 in snatch pulls using the same weight he had used for the 5, 4, 3 workout on February 2nd.

With incline dumbbell press, Daniel did 3x5 with a top weight of 63.5 kilos on February 1st, then 5,4,3 with heavier weight during this week from the blue phase.

And in the seated behind-the-neck press, he did exactly the same sets, reps, and weight during the February 1st green week and the February 15th blue week.

This was to help Daniel maintain a balance when he tapered. Yes, we needed to cut back in the weight room so he had more energy for throwing, but if we reduced his lifting too much, he could begin to feel sloppy and lose the healthy sense of tension in his body that he needed to throw far.

So, I used the alternative lifts to make sure he kept enough volume in his lifting to stay sharp. How much volume was that? I cannot say exactly. On the alternative lifts during the blue period, I went by feel. I trusted my eyes, I listened to what Daniel had to say, and I made any adjustments I considered necessary.

More slamming

Daniel's throwing during this blue phase consisted of two high-intensity sessions and two technical sessions. In the sample week, you can see the high-intensity sessions came on Monday (following the Sunday rest day) and Thursday (following the easy workout on Wednesday) so he would have plenty of energy to put into his throwing. On Monday, we did a slam session with 6 measured attempts. On Thursday, we did another slam session, but we did not measure the exact distance of his throws. During this blue period, Daniel was extremely consistent. He threw 69-70 meters in every slam session.

The other two throwing sessions each week were more focused on technique. I would ask him each session to produce 15-20 non-maximal full throws of at least 65 meters just trying to reinforce throwing with rhythm, and he almost always delivered.

Overall, I was happy with many aspects of the first half of our training plan. Daniel finished the first blue phase brutally strong and totally healthy. I hoped he might break Gerd Kanter's indoor world discus record of 69.51m at our competition in Växjö, but it did not happen. Daniel showed a lot of power, but he was not sharp and ended up fouling all six of his attempts, the farthest of which measured 68.82m.

But his ability to throw far indoors showed his capacity was high, and so I judged this phase of his training to be a success.

Foul!

I would like to comment, though, on the matter of fouling. I do not think a World Champion should foul so much, and it may be a weakness of mine as a coach that I did not push him more on this. During training, I always focused on coaching my athletes to throw far rather than coaching them to worry about fouling. I generally assumed that when they were throwing well with good technique, they would not foul, and luckily, Daniel rarely fouled in big competitions. But he occasionally lost his focus, as he did at the indoor meet, and started fouling, and this bothered me. So, it is possible that I needed to be harder on him about this in practice.

Second Yellow Period – 15th March to 29th May 2021

And now, the harder part

Daniel took one week of rest after the indoor discus competition before starting the second yellow phase on March 15th. If you look at the chart outlining the plan for the entire year, it shows this second yellow phase beginning on March 22nd. That would have been right after our annual trip to Leiria, Portugal, for the European Throwing Cup, but since the trip was canceled due to the pandemic, we began this phase a week sooner than planned.

There are parts of this second yellow phase which were typically the most physically challenging of the entire year. The sets and reps were similar to what we used during the first yellow phase, but the weights lifted were higher and more challenging as Daniel was usually in excellent shape by this time of the year and the weights used for each set were based on new lifting PBs Daniel achieved during the first yellow and green phases.

For example, during his first week of training in October, Daniel did 3x5 in back squats with 160, 180, and 200 kilos. In the first week of this second yellow phase, he again did 3x5 on back squats, but this time using 220, 230, and 240 kilos.

Because the beginning, middle, and end of this yellow phase were so different, I will describe each portion separately.

Beginning Weeks: 15th March to 4th April (Program 9 Base 4)

Okay, let's fix this!

As you can see from the March 15 sample week, we did only three weekly throwing sessions during the early portion of this yellow phase. I was not happy about Daniel fouling all his attempts at our indoor competition in Växjö, so I put a lot of drills, walk-through throws, and non-reverse throws into this phase of his program. I wanted him to take a lot of throws (30-40 a session) on balance and under control.

Daniel Ståhl Program 9 Base #4	15/03-21/03 2021	
SESSION 1	**SESSION 2**	
15-Mar		
Drills in the training hall plus very little throwing: Be warmed up at kl. 12.15 + VIDEO	**Warm up:** Bike 5-10min	
	Olympic Warmup: Snatch Routine	
	Lifting:	
	Snatch Pull / Box	3x5x165,170,175
	Back Squats	3x5x220,230,240
	Bench Press	3x5x155,165,175
	Leg Curl	3x10-12
	Adduction	3x12-15
	ABS & STABS: Upper, lower, rotation 3 sets each, DO IT!	
	Stretch: (Back, butt, hamstring, groin, hip flexor, chest)	
16-Mar		
Warm up: Jog 5-10min	**Cardio 60min**	
Hurdle walk or Running School: 5-10 hurdles, 5-10 ex/1-2x20-30mx5-10 ex.		
Fitness Warmup: Tommy Routine		
Throwing Discus: 2.0kg, 30-40 throws, walks, fulls NR, R. Many routines, controlled throws		
Stretch: (Back, butt, hamstring, groin, hip flexor, chest)		

17-Mar	
Cardio 60min (or FITNESS)	**Warm up:** Bike 5-10min
	Olympic Warmup: Snatch 3x3x60kg, Clean 3x3x100kg
	Lifting: **Push Press** 3x5x145,155,165
	Sumo Deadlift 3x5x250,265,280
	Press Behind Neck 3x5x90,95,100
	Reverse Fly 3x8-10
	Bent Over Row 3x8-10 or Lat Pull 3x8-10
	ABS & STABS: Upper, lower, rotation 3 sets each, DO IT!
	Stretch: (Back, butt, hamstring, groin, hip flexor, chest)
18-Mar	
Drills in the training hall plus very little throwing	**Cardio 60min**
19-Mar	
Warm up: Jog 5-10min	**Warm up:** Bike 5-10min
Hurdle walk or Running School: 5-10 hurdles, 5-10 ex/1-2x20-30mx5-10 ex.	**Olympic Warmup:** Clean Routine
Fitness Warmup: Tommy Routine	**Lifting:** **Clean Pull / Box** 3x5x180,185,190
Throwing Discus: 2.0kg, 30-40 throws, walks, fulls NR, R	**Front Squats** 3x5x155,160,165
Stretch: (Back, butt, hamstring, groin, hip flexor, chest)	**Incline DB Bench Press** 3x5x61,63.5,66
	Leg Curl 3x10-12
	Adduction 3x12-15
	ABS & STABS: Upper, lower, rotation 3 sets each, DO IT!
	Stretch: (Back, butt, hamstring, groin, hip flexor, chest)
20-Mar	
FITNESS: VH	**Cardio 60min**
21-Mar	
REST	REST

You may also notice we no longer included stand throws in Daniel's routine at this point. To be honest, for a thrower at Daniel's level, stands are not important. The better a thrower gets, the less they need to do partial movements, so it was not uncommon for Daniel to go right to walking fulls or fulls with a static start. When I planned a throwing session, I would assign a particular range of throws I wanted him to take (say 40-50), but the exact composition of those 40-50 throws was not set in stone. Sometimes, we began a session with some partial movements or drills. Other times, if we were excited about working on a certain aspect of his throw, we went directly to fulls.

A quick reset

During the first three weeks of this yellow phase, you can see we got away from our normal 2-2-1 rhythm and spread out three throwing and three lifting sessions over seven days. This is similar to what we did for the first three weeks when he began his training in October. The reasoning then was to take a little time to get him into shape before resuming our typical routine. Here in March, he was already in good shape, but the yellow phase is long, and so we had plenty of time to do a little reset before getting back to hard training.

Also, the reduced volume of lifting would give us more time and energy to focus on and hopefully correct this issue of fouling.

Even though Daniel lifted only three sessions in each of these introductory weeks, he still performed each of his main lifts (back squat, bench press, sumo deadlift, push press) and each of his alternative lifts (front squat, incline dumbbell press, snatch pull, behind the neck press) once. We made this possible by having him do three of those lifts each session, and we even added an extra session of pulls to his third lifting day. We were able to do this because we kept the intensity and volume low during this three-week segment, though not as low as the October yellow phase. Then, we kept Daniel's lifts in the 60 percent range. In this March yellow phase, his lifts were closer to 70 percent, give or take 5 percent.

You have been warned!

Notice the notation "Fitness: VH" on March 20th. The "VH" stands for me, Vésteinn Hafsteinsson. This was to let Daniel know I would be running the training session that day. As I explained, our Wednesday and Saturday workouts usually consisted of mobility/stability work and a bit of cardio, and I liked to let the athletes manage those on their own. This way, they got a break from me and it was also good for them to take responsibility for their own training at times. However, Daniel did not love doing mobility/stability work, and so sometimes I had to take over managing those sessions.

Middle Weeks: 5th April to 2nd May

5th April to 11th April (Program 10 Base 5)

Back to the plan…for a while

This middle section of the second yellow phase was meant to be very similar to the November-December section of the first yellow phase. If you compare the lifting Daniel did during the sample week of November 23rd to the sample week from the second yellow phase above, you will see his routine was almost exactly the same. The only difference was that in some of the exercises he was moving heavier weights after several months of hard training.

On November 23rd, for example, Daniel did 5x5 in back squats with a top weight of 230 kilograms. On April 5th, he once again did 5x5 in back squats, this time with a top weight of 255 kilos.

On November 26th, he did 5x5 in bench press with a best set of 165 kilos. On April 8th, he did 5x5 with a best set of 172.5 kilos.

You may notice when you compare those two training weeks that the weight Daniel used on incline dumbbell bench press, push press, and sumo deadlift did not increase. This was a result of us trying to maintain a balance in Daniel's training. Remember, a thrower should never be so exhausted from lifting as to be unable to function in the ring, so we chose certain lifts to periodize and others to use mainly for volume. On the volume lifts, it was not so important to keep increasing the weight. The focus was on getting in the work.

During this period, we also returned to throwing four times per week, with the harder sessions coming on Mondays (with the discus) and Fridays (with the Denfi tool), as was typical during the November-December yellow phase.

For a while, it appeared all was going according to plan. Then, we ran into some difficulty. The return to hard lifting and throwing made it difficult for Daniel to find his feeling and rhythm with the discus during the months of March and April of 2021.

Daniel Ståhl Program 10 Base # 5	05/04-02/05 2021
SESSION 1	**SESSION 2**
5-Apr	
Warm up: Jog 5-10min	**Warm up:** Bike 5-10min
Hurdle walk or Running School: 5-10 hurdles, 5-10 ex/1-2x20-30mx5-10 ex.	**Olympic Warmup:** Sit Snatch 3x3x60,70,80kg
	Lifting:
Fitness Warmup: Tommy Routine	**Back Squats** 5x5x70-80% = 225,240,255,225,225
Throwing Discus: 2.0kg, 5 stand, 5 walks, fulls 5-10 NR, 10-15 R	**Incline DB Press** 5x5x70-80% = 56,58.5,61,63.5,56
Stretch: (Back, butt, hamstring, groin, hip flexor, chest)	Bent Over Row 3x8-10 or Lat Pull 3x8-10
	Leg Curl 3x10-12
If you feel like throwing far, then we will do it on this day	**ABS & STABS:** Upper, lower, rotation 3 sets each, DO IT!

6-Apr	
Warm up: Jog 5-10min	**Warm up:** Bike 5-10min
Hurdle walk or Running School: 5-10 hurdles, 5-10 ex/1-2x20-30mx5-10 ex.	**Olympic Warmup:** Clean Gymnastics
Fitness Warmup: Tommy Routine	**Lifting:** **Snatch Pull / Box** **3x5x120-130% = 180,185,190**
Throwing Discus: 2.0kg, 5-10 walks, 5-10 S&T, 10 NR, 10-15 R	**Push Press** **4x5x70-80% = 145,155,165,145**
Stretch: (Back, butt, hamstring, groin, hip flexor, chest)	Reverse Fly 3x8-10
	Adduction 3x12-15
	ABS & STABS: Upper, lower, rotation 3 sets each, DO IT!
7-Apr	
Warm up: Jog 5-10min	**REST (cardio)**
Hurdle walk or Running School: 5-10 hurdles, 5-10 ex/1-2x20-30mx5-10 ex.	
Gymnastics, medicine ball, fitness	
Rehab, Prehab	
Extra Stretch	
Cardio	
8-Apr	
Warm up: Jog 5-10min	**Warm up:** Bike 5-10min
Hurdle walk or Running School: 5-10 hurdles, 5-10 ex/1-2x20-30mx5-10 ex.	**Olympic Warmup:** Sit Clean 3x3x100,110,120kg
	Lifting:
Fitness Warmup: Tommy Routine	**Bench Press** **5x5x70-80% = 50,157.5,165,172.5,150**
Throwing Discus: 2.0kg, 5-10 walks, 5-10 S&T, 10 NR, 10-15 R	**Front Squats** **3x5x70-80% = 155,165,175**
Stretch: (Back, butt, hamstring, groin, hip flexor, chest)	Bent Over Row 3x8-10 or Lat Pull 3x8-10
	Leg Curl 3x10-12
	ABS & STABS: Upper, lower, rotation 3 sets each, DO IT!

9-Apr	
Warm up: Jog 5-10min	**Warm up:** Bike 5-10min
Hurdle walk or Running School: 5-10 hurdles, 5-10 ex/1-2x20-30mx5-10 ex.	**Olympic Warmup:** Snatch Gymnastics
	Lifting:
Fitness Warmup: Tommy Routine	**Sumo Deadlift** 4x5x65-70% = 260,270,280,260
Throwing Denfi 2.5kg-3.1kg: 30-40 throws 15-20 NR, 15-20 R	**Press Behind Neck/Seated** 3x5x70-80% = 90,97.5,105
Stretch: (Back, butt, hamstring, groin, hip flexor, chest)	Reverse Fly 3x8-10
	Adduction 3x12-15
	ABS & STABS: Upper, lower, rotation 3 sets each, DO IT!
10-Apr	
Warm up: Jog 5-10min	**REST (cardio)**
Hurdle walk or Running School: 5-10 hurdles, 5-10 ex/1-2x20-30mx5-10 ex.	
Gymnastics, medicine ball, fitness	
Rehab, Prehab	
Extra Stretch	
Cardio	
11-Apr	
REST	**REST**

This was a difficult situation for both of us, and it caused me to revise Daniel's training plan.

Pursuing perfection

It may sound crazy, but even though Daniel threw seventy meters at an indoor training session over the winter and showed great capacity at the indoor competition in Växjö, I was not happy with his technique.

During a typical session in March and April, Daniel would look good on easy, walk-through throws. He would look good while he stayed under control on his non-reverse throws. But, as soon as he hit the accelerator and tried to throw far, his technique fell apart.

The main issue was at the beginning of the sprint phase as he turned out of the back of the ring. When Daniel's left knee bent and his right knee began to sweep towards the center of the ring, he leaned backward just a bit, causing him to rise up during the non-support phase. This upset his balance and negatively affected the orbit of the disc. The high point of his orbit would come too early, his weight would shift to his left leg during his finish, and he would scoop the discus.

Daniel is so big and strong he could sometimes throw over seventy meters with this flaw, but we both knew he could throw even farther if we could correct it--so we tried, but without success.

And the situation might have been made harder by the fact that Daniel was thinking deeply about his technique. This was actually a sign of maturity. He was taking ownership of his technical development rather than simply doing what I asked him to do every day without question. But, at that moment, thinking harder about his technique was not helping him to fix his flaws--it only made his inability to fix them more frustrating for him.

When we watched film together, we both saw he needed to lean more into the middle as he began his sprint. This was a simple adjustment, but he could not feel how to make it.

As a coach, I have to say these times were the most exhausting. Daniel and I agreed on the adjustment he needed to make. We both knew what was possible if he made the adjustment. He was working hard to make the adjustment. But he simply could not do it.

Several times that spring, I got out of bed at 2:00 a.m. to watch film, trying to crack the code which would allow him to solve this issue. I even wondered if I had lost the ability to connect with someone as young as Daniel. When I first started coaching, I had just retired as a professional thrower and was not much older than the athletes I trained. But I am thirty years older than Daniel, and I worried this might be too big of a gap for me to reach across.

These are the kind of thoughts that come into your head when you know you have an athlete capable of winning the Olympics, maybe even breaking the world record if you can help them reach their maximum potential. Those possibilities brought out the Icelandic volcano in me.

I know these are First World problems. We were very lucky during Covid times that our facility in Sweden was never locked down. We stayed healthy and were able to work hard with no interruptions. My wife Anna always loved and supported me, as did my children. I got paid to work with some of the best athletes in the world.

And yet, I would get so wrapped up in pursuing the next achievement that it often felt like disaster was just around the corner.

As long as I'm awake...

During one 2:00 a.m. film session, I put together six of Daniel's best throws ever, all over 70 meters. Guess what? His technique looked like shit in those also.

This is something which happened a few times over the years. When I couldn't sleep because Gerd or Daniel or Joachim was struggling with a technical issue, I would search for the solution by looking at videos of big throws from earlier in their careers. But surprisingly, the video of those throws never matched my memory. I always recalled great throws like Daniel's 66.89m in 2014 as breakthrough moments where everything came together just right. But then, when I'd go back and watch the video maybe a couple of years later, I would always be disappointed by how terrible I thought their technique looked. It was the same for me when I was competing. I'd get someone to film me, and whenever I made a far throw I couldn't wait to get home and pop the tape into the VCR. But then, when I watched it, I always thought I looked like shit!

What it comes down to is speed. When a thrower finds a comfortable rhythm and is focused and not thinking about too much, they can move quickly and throw far even if their technique is not perfect.

This is why I rarely filmed my athletes in practice once the summer season began. At that point, it was time to put a lock on their technique and just feel it and do it.

Certainly, film study is an important part of coaching the throws. But you must keep it in perspective.

Back to Daniel. I showed him the film of his six best throws, all six on the same screen, and he said, "Well, we are not doing that bad!"

I asked him, "Why then are we throwing like shit?"

He said, "Well, my system is tired, and there is a lot going on in my head."

I said, "Yes, we both need to relax, and you need to clear your head, so we will focus on one key: you will drive across the ring without jumping up."

To help with this, we began watching film of the 66.89m throw from 2014. It was the throw that put him on the map, a world lead, and a huge PB. We noticed his technique at the back of the ring was simpler then. He used a shorter backswing, with very little weight shifted to the right leg. In the years since, we tried to maximize the advantage of Daniel's enormous wingspan by extending his backswing, which required him to shift more weight to his right leg. Somehow, in the spring of 2021, this was upsetting his balance. Ideally, we would find a way to keep the long windup but also allow him to achieve a stable entry into the throw.

Shoulders over hips

My basic concept of discus technique is that you are walking and turning with your arms out and your shoulders square over your hips. You stay upright with no diving as if you have a cup of coffee on each shoulder and are trying not to spill.

The windup and entry are an important part of this. Many throwers give themselves no chance to stay on balance through the throw because they are already unstable as they wind the discus back.

I began to suspect Daniel's struggle with his technique was due to him leaning too much with his upper body during his windup rather than staying upright with his shoulders and hips square. This threw off his entry and resulted in him jumping and rising up as he ran to the middle.

For him to run the ring more efficiently--more horizontally--he needed to find the same sense of balance in his long windup that he'd had using a shorter windup in 2014.

To make this easier, I decided to change our training plan in the final section of this yellow phase--basically the month of May.

Second Yellow Period Final Segment: 3rd May to 29th May

3rd May to 12th May (Program 11 Base 6)

We adjust

As you can see from the May 3rd sample week, I made a big change to the structure of Daniel's training at this time. During May of 2021, Daniel's program looked like this:

Day 1: A light technique session in the morning, with 10-15 walkthroughs from a static starting position, trying to capture the feeling he had in the throw from 2014. This was followed by 5-10 full throws from the static position, then between 5-10 non-reverse full throws using the slightly modified windup we came up with. We would finish with 5 full throws with a reverse, also from our modified windup. In between throws, we would do a few drills and look at the video. This entire session would take approximately 45 minutes.

In the afternoon, instead of lifting as we normally would, he had a slam session starting with 5 walkthroughs, doing his best to find the feel of his 2014 technique. He would then take 6 warmup throws, followed by 6-12 full throws with as little fouling as possible.

Day 2: In the morning, we did another light session with almost no throwing, just drills and video--basically an analysis of Monday's slam session. During this period, if he was tired from the slam session, we would just do a bit of cardio or only watch film.

In the afternoon, he did bench and squats, but at a lighter intensity than we would have normally done during this part of the yellow phase. Usually, the May yellow period would be very similar to the December yellow period, only he would be using heavier weights in May because he would be stronger by then. But, on December 7th, for example, Daniel did 3x5 on back squats with 220, 237.5, and 255 kilos, and as you can see from the May 3rd sample week, he once again did 3x5, but with less weight: 200, 215, and 230 kilos.

Daniel Ståhl Program 11 Base # 6	03/05-12/05 2021
SESSION 1	**SESSION 2**
3-May	
REST	**Warm up:** Jog 5-10min
(wake-up call Daniel Ståhl way, cardio, drills, video)	**Throwing Discus:** 2.0kg, 3-5 stand, 5-10 walks, 4-5 fulls NR, 10-12 fulls R
	Stretch: (Back, butt, hamstring, groin, hip flexor, chest)
4-May	
Cardio 60 min (plus video/drills, few throws)	**Warm up:** Bike 5-10min
	Olympic Warmup: Sit Clean 3,2,1x100,120,140 or Snatch 3,2,1x70,80,90
	Lifting:
	Back Squats 3x5x67.5-77.5% = 145,155,165 **or Front Squats** 3x5x62.5-72.5% = 140,150,160
	Bench Press 3x5x67.5-77.5% = 145,155,165 **or** **Incline D.P.** 3x5x67.5-77.5% = 53.5,58.5,63.5
	Bent Over Row 3x8-10 or Lat Pull 3x8-10
	Leg Curl 3x10-12
	ABS & STABS: Upper, lower, rotation 3 sets each, DO IT!

	5-May	
Warm up: Jog 5-10min	**Warm up:** Bike 5-10min	
	Lifting:	
Hurdle walk or Running School: 5-10 hurdles, 5-10 ex/1-2x20-30mx5-10 ex.	**Push Press** 3x5x67.5-77.5% = 140,150,160 or **Press B. Neck** 3x5x67.5-77.5% = 90,95,100	
Fitness Warmup: Tommy Routine	**Sumo DL** 3x5x62.5-72.5% = 250,265,280 or **Snatch Pull/Box** 3x5x62.5-72.5% = 170,180,190	
Throwing Discus: 2.0kg, 5 stand, 5-10 walks, 10 fulls NR, 10-15 fulls R (routine 60-65m)	Reverse Fly 3x8-10	
Stretch: (Back, butt, hamstring, groin, hip flexor, chest)	Adduction 3x12-15	
NO FOULS	**ABS & STABS:** Upper, lower, rotation 3 sets each, DO IT!	
	6-May	
REST	REST	
	7-May	
Cardio 60min	REST	
	8-May	
REST	**Warm up:** Jog 5-10min	
(wake-up call Daniel Ståhl way, cardio, drills, video)	**Throwing Discus:** 2.0kg, 3-5 stand, 5-10 walks, 4-5 fulls NR, 10-12 fulls R	
	Stretch: (Back, butt, hamstring, groin, hip flexor, chest)	
	9-May	
Cardio 60 min (plus video/drills, few throws)	**Warm up:** Bike 5-10min	
	Olympic Warmup: Sit Clean 3,2,1x100,120,140 or Snatch 3,2,1x70,80,90	
	Lifting: **Bench Press** 5,4,3x75-85% = 160,170,180+ or **Incline D.P.** 5,4,3x75-85% = 58.5,63.5,68.5+	
	Bent Over Row 3x8-10 or Lat Pull 3x8-10	
	Leg Curl 3x10-12	
	ABS & STABS: Upper, lower, rotation 3 sets each, DO IT!	

10-May	
Warm up: Jog 5-10min	**Warm up:** Bike 5-10min
	Lifting:

Fitness Warmup: Tommy Routine	**Sumo**
	     5,4,3x70-80% = 270,285,300 or
	 Snatch Pull/Box
	     5,4,3x70-80% = 180,190,200

Throwing Discus: 2.0kg, 5 stand, 5-10 walks, 10 fulls NR, 10-15 fulls R (routine 60-65m)	Reverse Fly 3x8-10
Stretch: (Back, butt, hamstring, groin, hip flexor, chest)	Adduction 3x12-15
NO FOULS	**ABS & STABS:** Upper, lower, rotation 3 sets each, DO IT!
11-May	
REST	**REST**
12-May	
Cardio 60min	**REST**

This may seem to go against what I said about how important it is to keep a thrower strong throughout the entire season, especially a big guy like Daniel who could lose his feel and start feeling sloppy if we didn't keep enough volume and intensity in his routine. You will see in a few pages how hard we worked to maintain Daniel's strength levels throughout June and July as he traveled and competed, and even during our final training camp before the Games. So, why "pull the plug" on lifting intensity in May?

Because I made the decision that we needed to focus his energy on achieving his best throwing technique during this time. As I said, an athlete must put a lock on their technique once the heavy competition season begins so they can stay out of their head and throw far on rhythm and feel. Once we reached the last week of May, Daniel would be competing constantly, so if we were going to adjust his form, we had to do it before then.

And if we were going to spend extra energy on throwing, we would need to compensate by reducing the amount of energy he would use in the weight room.

Luckily, Daniel was extremely strong after all the hard work he had done over the previous seven months. This gave us the luxury of focusing on throwing for a few weeks. Also, when we made this adjustment in May, we still had time to get back to our normal volume and intensity well before the Olympics.

You will also notice that during this period, I gave Daniel a choice in his main lifts each session. I did so because with the focus on throwing, what was important in the weight room was getting through the sets and reps. If he felt tired on a certain day, or if I thought he looked tired, we had the option of substituting a less strenuous exercise like front squats for back squats or seated behind-the-neck press for push press.

Day 3: In the morning, we would do a pretty easy session of 20-25 full throws with a reverse, landing them somewhere between 60-65 meters.

In the afternoon, he would do his pulls or sumo deadlift and a press.

Day 4: This was a day of rest.

Day 5: Cardio in the morning and then rest. The two rest days would allow him to recover completely from the previous three days of training.

After five days, we would go back to the Day 1 schedule and repeat this sequence.

You will notice on the second squat/bench day and the second push press/sumo day, we switched from 3x5 to 5,4,3 with a little bit higher intensity. Going heavier every other session allowed us to maintain Daniel's strength levels without wearing him down too much. And the weights he lifted during this May yellow phase were still lighter than during the corresponding December yellow phase. On December 14th, for example, Daniel did 5,4,3 in back squats at 230, 250, and 270 kilos. As you can see, on May 9th he did 5,4,3 with 225, 240, and 255 kilos, though the "+" attached to the 255 means that he could go a little higher if he was feeling good.

So, this was our pattern of training for the rest of the month, and I was happy with the results. Daniel made progress with his technique, and at his opening meet in Helsingborg on May 22nd he went 69.71m. A week later in Växjö, he had a 73.83m foul and a best mark of 69.11m. This made me feel better about putting a lock on his technique for the summer.

Next came the hardest period of the entire season.

Second Green Period - 30ᵗʰ May to 13ᵗʰ July 2021

The grind

This was by far the most difficult phase to plan. We needed to allow Daniel to compete well during a tremendously busy part of the year but to do it in a way which did not detract from our ultimate goal of winning Olympic gold. If we cut Daniel's volume of training too early, he might end up feeling sloppy and out of shape by the time we traveled to Japan to begin our final phase of training before the Games. At that point, it would be too late to restore his good feeling. On the other hand, if we kept the volume and intensity of training too high, we risked exhausting or even injuring him with very little time to recover before the most important competition of his career.

The way we managed this phase is a bit complicated, so I will go through it day by day.

Daniel Ståhl Program 12 Strength # 2	30/05-27/06 2021
SESSION 1	**SESSION 2**
30-May	
Cardio 60min (plus video/drills, few throws)	**Warm up:** Bike 5-10min
	Olympic Warmup: Sit Clean 3,2,1x100,120,140 Snatch 3,2,1x70,80,90

	Lifting:
	Back Squats
	    3x5x62.5-72.5% = 200,215,230 or
	Front Squats
	    3x5x62.5-72.5% = 140,150,160

	Bench Press
	    3x5x67.5-77.5% = 145,155,165 or
	Incline D.P.
	    3x5x67.5-77.5% = 53.5,58.5,63.5

	Bent Over Row 3x8-10 or Lat Pull 3x8-10
	Leg Curl 3x10-12
	ABS & STABS: Upper, lower, rotation 3 sets each, DO IT!
31-May	
Warm up: Jog 5-10min	**Warm up:** Bike 5-10min

Hurdle walk or Running School: 5-10 hurdles, 5-10 ex/1-2x20-30mx5-10 ex.	**Lifting:**
	Push Press
	    3x5x67.5-77.5% = 140,150,160 or
	Press B. Neck
	    3x5x67.5-77.5% = 90,95,100

Fitness Warmup: Tommy Routine	**Sumo DL**
	    3x5x62.5-72.5% = 250,265,280 or
	Snatch Pull/Box
	    3x5x62.5-72.5% = 170,180,190

Throwing Discus: 2.0kg, 5 stand, 5-10 walks, 10 fulls NR, 10-15 fulls R (routine 60-65m)	Reverse Fly 3x8-10
Stretch: (Back, butt, hamstring, groin, hip flexor, chest)	Adduction 3x12-15
NO FOULS	**ABS & STABS:** Upper, lower, rotation 3 sets each, DO IT!
1-Jun	
REST	REST

May 30

We begin the day after the competition in Växjö, where Daniel fouled a 73.83m throw. Obviously, his capacity at this point was very high, and we were excited moving forward. In the morning, we did a session of cardio, which for Daniel meant walking 60-90 minutes. He used a lot of energy when he competed, so we usually did not throw the day after. We might do a few drills and some video study, but it was important for him to recover fully. For the afternoon session, he got to choose between cleans and snatches as a warmup. As I mentioned earlier, the Olympic lifts were not among Daniel's core lifts because for a man of his size, throwing is very taxing, and trying to crowd throwing and Olympic lifting into each week would be too much for him.

That said, Daniel enjoyed doing cleans and snatches, and they helped to keep him limber. Sets of 3x2 with a light load as a warmup got him ready to lift but did not require much energy.

For his main lifts, Daniel could choose back or front squats, and bench presses or incline dumbbell presses. Giving him a choice in his lifts was especially important during this second green phase, as traveling and competing would sometimes sap his energy, and letting him substitute front squats for back squats, for example, gave him a bit of extra confidence and motivation when he was tired.

On this day, he did 3x5 at between 67.5 and 77.5 percent for bench press and 3x5 at 62.5-72.5% for squats. Throughout this phase, we would alternate between 3x5 and 5-4-3 on the main lifts. On the first two lifting days of this week, we had him do 3x5 as he was recovering from the competition in Växjö. As you will see, the next time he performed these lifts, it would be 5-4-3. For the 5-4-3 sessions, we generally stayed in the 75-85% range for upper body lifts and 70-80% for squats and sumo deadlifts.

The key on the 5-4-3 days was the set of 3. If we could maintain a fairly normal level of volume during this phase and also work up to a heavy set of

3 on the 5-4-3 days, I was confident we could keep Daniel's strength levels where they needed to be in spite of all the traveling and competing.

You will notice for some sessions during this phase, I again added a plus mark to the suggested weights. On June 3rd, for example, the suggested weights for back squats were 225, 240, and 255+. This gave me the flexibility to adjust the intensity of certain sessions. Though the listed percentages for back squats and deadlifts never went higher than 80% during this period, I wanted to always take the opportunity to do the set of 3 at a weight higher than 80% when possible. There were some days when we could not because Daniel was worn out from traveling and competing, but I always wanted to give Daniel the option to go heavier on days when he felt up to it. For example, if he was feeling energized and strong, he might go as high as 280 kilos on back squats when my suggested weight was 255+. This approach allowed us to keep him fresh, healthy, and strong during this time.

And notice that on both the 3x5 and 5-4-3 days, the total number of reps was not high--either 15 or 12. This made it easier to get his workouts in even when he was on the road.

May 31

Our first session on this day began with a warmup, either hurdle walks or running school, followed by an easy throwing session. "Running school" consisted of the typical exercises you would find in most versions of a "dynamic warmup," things like high knees and skipping. Another warmup Daniel did sometimes was the "Tommy Routine," which, as I mentioned earlier, was a series of gymnastics exercises put together for Daniel by our physiotherapist, Tommy Eriksson.

You will notice I wrote "NO FOULS" for the throwing session. As I described earlier, Daniel showed huge capacity at our competition in Växjö. This indicated our training up to that point had been successful. All the hard work from October to May was money in the bank. Now, in order to withdraw some of that money, he would need to stay in the ring, so throwing without fouling would be part of his routine in training.

The lifting session was 3x5 in the 67.5-77.5% range for push press and 62.5-72.5% for sumo deadlifts. We put sumo deadlifts on this day as Daniel preferred to do them two days before a competition.

June 1

This was a day of rest before competing in Göteborg.

Daniel Ståhl Program 12 Strength # 2	30/05-27/06 2021
SESSION 1	**SESSION 2**
2-Jun	
REST **(wake-up call Daniel Ståhl way, cardio, drills, video)**	**Warm up:** Jog 5-10min
	Throwing Discus: 2.0kg, Your warmup before the meet, D.S. own routine
	Stretch: (Back, butt, hamstring, groin, hip flexor, chest)
3-Jun	
Cardio 60 min (plus video/drills, few throws)	**Warm up:** Bike 5-10min
	Olympic Warmup: Sit Clean 3,2,1x100,120,140 or Snatch 3,2,1x70,80,90

	Lifting:
	 Back Squats
	         5,4,3x70-80% = 225,240,255+ or
	 Front Squats
	         5,4,3x70-80% = 155,165,175+

	Bench Press
	         5,4,3x75-85% = 160,170,180+ or
	 Incline D.P.
	         5,4,3x75-85% = 58.5,63.5,68.5+

	Bent Over Row 3x8-10 or Lat Pull 3x8-10
	Leg Curl 3x10-12
	ABS & STABS: Upper, lower, rotation 3 sets each, DO IT!

4-Jun	
Warm up: Jog 5-10min	**Warm up:** Bike 5-10min

Hurdle walk or Running School: 5-10 hurdles, 5-10 ex/1-2x20-30mx5-10 ex.	**Lifting:**
	Push Press
	    5,4,3x75-85% = 155,165,175 or
	Press B. Neck
	    5,4,3x75-85% = 100,105,110

Fitness Warmup: Tommy Routine	**Sumo DL**
	    5,4,3x70-80% = 270,285,300 or
	Snatch Pull/Box
	    5,4,3x70-80% = 180,190,200

Throwing Discus: 2.0kg, 5 stand, 5-10 walks, 10 fulls NR, 10-15 fulls R (routine 60-65m)	Reverse Fly 3x8-10
Stretch: (Back, butt, hamstring, groin, hip flexor, chest)	Adduction 3x12-15
NO FOULS	**ABS & STABS:** Upper, lower, rotation 3 sets each, DO IT!
5-Jun	
Cardio 60 min	**REST**
6-Jun	
REST	**REST**

June 2

In the morning, we did a "wake-up call," which for Daniel was almost always a walk. Most of my throwers preferred some kind of "wake-up call" on the day of a competition as a way to prime their nervous system. Fanny liked to take a few throws for her wake-up call, but a big guy like Daniel must be careful about conserving energy, so walking was best for him.

At the competition that evening, he took his usual warmup of one non-reverse full throw from a static start and one non-reverse full throw with a full windup. At major competitions like the European or World Championships, athletes are given the opportunity to take throws at a warm-up track before they are transported into the stadium, but Daniel never did. As long as he got two or three throws in the ring prior to the competition, he was ready to go. The goal when taking warmup throws was to put his technique together. I didn't want him going too easy, so he typically threw

66-67 meters in warmups. There is also no need to try to set a world record while warming up, and Daniel was very good at finding the right balance. He did not need to prove to himself that he was a good thrower by setting records before the competition began. In fact, I have seen him throw poorly during warmups and then compete very well. This is one of the qualities which allowed him to be successful in major championships.

Daniel's best measured attempt in the Göteborg meeting was 66.81m in dead conditions--no wind. He also had three fouls over 70 meters. His rhythm was not there yet, and I was not happy about the fouling, but he was not flying out of the ring to throw far, so I knew we were close.

June 3

The morning session was normal for the day after a competition--cardio only. In the afternoon, Daniel did 5-4-3 at 75-85% on bench presses and 70-80% on squats. We would usually do 3x5 the day after a meeting, but I wanted to stick to the pattern of alternating between 3x5 and 5-4-3. As I said, the heavy set of 3 at the end of the 5-4-3 routine was vital to keeping his strength levels high, and I did not want him to miss those sets, so we changed our usual approach and got the 5-4-3 in on this day.

June 4

We began the day with an easy throwing session where Daniel focused on making "routine" throws with no fouls.

The lifting session was 5-4-3 in the 75-85% range for push press and 70-80% for sumo deadlift.

June 5 and June 6

We gave Daniel two days of rest before the competition in Turku, Finland. Daniel's mother is from Finland, and he always loved throwing there, so I gave him extra rest to increase his chances of performing well. This is a variation on our usual routine, but I tried to set it up this way a couple of times per season for the meets Daniel cared about most.

On the morning of the first rest day, June 5th, he did a bit of cardio--his normal 90-minute walk.

We usually did this on the morning of the first day when he had two days of rest because it is easy for a big guy to get stiff during two consecutive days off, and the walk loosened him up.

Daniel Ståhl Program 12 Strength # 2	30/05-27/06 2021
SESSION 1	**SESSION 2**
7-Jun	
REST	**Warm up:** Jog 5-10min
(wake-up call Daniel Ståhl way, cardio, drills, video)	**Throwing Discus:** 2.0kg, Your warmup before the meet, D.S. own routine
	Stretch: (Back, butt, hamstring, groin, hip flexor, chest)
8-Jun	
REST	**Cardio 60min**
9-Jun	
Warm up: Jog 5-10min	**Warm up:** Bike 5-10min
Hurdle walk or Running School: 5-10 hurdles, 5-10 ex/1-2x20-30mx5-10 ex.	**Olympic Warmup:** Sit Clean 3,2,1x100,120,140 or Snatch 3,2,1x70,80,90

Fitness Warmup: Tommy Routine	**Lifting:**
	Back Squats
	    3x5x62.5-72.5% = 200,215,230 or
	Front Squats
	    3x5x62.5-72.5% = 140,150,160

Throwing Discus: 2.0kg, 5 stand, 5-10 walks, 10 fulls NR, 10-15 fulls R (routine 60-65m)	**Bench Press**
	    3x5x67.5-77.5% = 145,155,165 or
	Incline D.P.
	    3x5x67.5-77.5% = 53.5,58.5,63.5

Stretch: (Back, butt, hamstring, groin, hip flexor, chest)	Bent Over Row 3x8-10 or Lat Pull 3x8-10
NO FOULS	Leg Curl 3x10-12
	ABS & STABS: Upper, lower, rotation 3 sets each, DO IT!

10-Jun	
Cardio 60min (plus video/drills, few throws)	**Warm up:** Bike 5-10min

	Lifting:
	Push Press
	    3x5x67.5-77.5% = 140,150,160 or
	Press B. Neck
	    3x5x67.5-77.5% = 90,95,100

	Sumo DL
	    3x5x62.5-72.5% = 250,265,280 or
	Snatch Pull/Box
	    3x5x62.5-72.5% = 170,180,190

	Reverse Fly 3x8-10
	Adduction 3x12-15
	ABS & STABS: Upper, lower, rotation 3 sets each, DO IT!

11-Jun	
Warm up: Jog 5-10min	**Cardio 60min**
Hurdle walk or Running School: 5-10 hurdles, 5-10 ex/1-2x20-30mx5-10 ex.	
Fitness Warmup: Tommy Routine	
Throwing Discus: 2.0kg, 5 stand, 5-10 walks, 10 fulls NR, 10-15 fulls R (routine 60-65m)	
Stretch: (Back, butt, hamstring, groin, hip flexor, chest)	
NO FOULS	

12-Jun	
REST	REST

13-Jun	
REST	**Warm up:** Jog 5-10min
(wake-up call Daniel Ståhl way, cardio, drills, video)	**Throwing Discus:** 2.0kg, Your warmup before the meet, D.S. own routine
	Stretch: (Back, butt, hamstring, groin, hip flexor, chest)

14-Jun	
REST	**Cardio 60min**

June 7

In the morning, he did his wake-up call--another walk--and that night, he competed in Turku. He was still working to find his rhythm but fouled only twice and finished with a best mark of 68.11m. There was a tailwind during this competition, so I was happy with his distance and also with the fact that he had four legal throws.

June 8

We did not do a morning session, as Daniel was traveling back from Finland. In the evening, he did cardio to get loose.

June 9

We had an easy throwing practice in the morning, followed by an afternoon lifting session where he did 3x5 on his main lifts, 67.5-77.5% on bench press and 62.5-72.5% on squats.

June 10

We did cardio only on this morning because we had an extra day between the meetings at Turku and Sollentuna. To maintain the rhythm of our training, we needed to do two throwing and two lifting sessions between each competition, and we were able to spread those sessions over three days this time.

The afternoon lift was 3x5 at 67.5-77.5% for push press and 62.5-72.5% for sumo deadlift.

June 11

We had another light throwing session in the morning and did only cardio in the afternoon because we had already done our two lifting sessions. I mentioned earlier that Daniel preferred to do sumo deadlift two days prior to competing, but three days before works as well, and in this case, lifting on the 9th and 10th fit better into our schedule.

June 12

This was a day of rest before our meeting at Sollentuna.

June 13

The day began with a normal wakeup call. That evening, Daniel competed in Sollentuna. He won with a throw of 68.03m and looked like he was getting closer to finding his best rhythm. As in Turku, there was a tailwind in Sollentuna, so 68.03m was a pretty good throw.

June 14

He rested in the morning and did cardio in the afternoon.

Daniel Ståhl Program 12 Strength # 2	30/05-27/06 2021
SESSION 1	**SESSION 2**
15-Jun	
Warm up: Jog 5-10min	**Warm up:** Bike 5-10min
Hurdle walk or Running School: 5-10 hurdles, 5-10 ex/1-2x20-30mx5-10 ex.	**Olympic Warmup:** Sit Clean 3,2,1x100,120,140 or Snatch 3,2,1x70,80,90

Fitness Warmup: Tommy Routine	**Lifting:**
	Back Squats
	    5,4,3x70-80% = 225,240,255+ or
	Front Squats
	    5,4,3x70-80% = 155,165,175+

Throwing Discus: 2.0kg, 5 stand, 5-10 walks, 10 fulls NR, 10-15 fulls R (routine 60-65m)	**Bench Press**
	    5,4,3x75-85% = 160,170,180+ or
	Incline D.P.
	    5,4,3x75-85% = 58.5,63.5,68.5+

Stretch: (Back, butt, hamstring, groin, hip flexor, chest)	Bent Over Row 3x8-10 or Lat Pull 3x8-10
NO FOULS	Leg Curl 3x10-12
	ABS & STABS: Upper, lower, rotation 3 sets each, DO IT!

16-Jun	
Warm up: Jog 5-10min	**Warm up:** Bike 5-10min

Hurdle walk or Running School: 5-10 hurdles, 5-10 ex/1-2x20-30mx5-10 ex.	**Lifting:**
	Push Press
	    5,4,3x75-85% = 155,165,175 or
	Press B. Neck
	    5,4,3x75-85% = 100,105,110

Fitness Warmup: Tommy Routine	**Sumo DL**
	    5,4,3x70-80% = 270,285,300 or
	Snatch Pull/Box
	    5,4,3x70-80% = 180,190,200

Throwing Discus: 2.0kg, 5 stand, 5-10 walks, 10 fulls NR, 10-15 fulls R (routine 60-65m)	Reverse Fly 3x8-10
Stretch: (Back, butt, hamstring, groin, hip flexor, chest)	Adduction 3x12-15
NO FOULS	**ABS & STABS:** Upper, lower, rotation 3 sets each, DO IT!
17-Jun	
Cardio 60min	**REST**
18-Jun	
REST	**Warm up:** Jog 5-10min
(wake-up call Daniel Ståhl way, cardio, drills, video)	**Throwing Discus:** 2.0kg, 3-5 stand, 5-10 walks, 4-5 fulls NR, 10-12 fulls R
	Stretch: (Back, butt, hamstring, groin, hip flexor, chest)

June 15

We did our usual morning throwing session, then a 5-4-3 lift in the afternoon at 75-85% for bench press and 70-80% in squats.

June 16

We had another morning throwing session and an afternoon lift doing 5-4-3 at 75-85% for push press and 70-80% for sumo deadlift.

June 17

This was a cardio session in the morning, then rest. No afternoon session.

June 18

As I have said, the body and mind respond best when an athlete can maintain a rhythm in their training. I described earlier how, during the winter and spring, we generally adhered to a schedule of 2-2-1, 2-2-1, rest. The week began with two training sessions on consecutive days, followed by a day with only one session. We repeated that pattern, then rested on Sunday.

Ideally, we would have maintained the 2-2-1 pattern during the competition season, but the demands of travel and the need to recover after competing made this a difficult task. Still, I took every effort to keep my athletes on a rhythm of training and competing that allowed them to feel confident and comfortable.

After Sollentuna on the 13th, Daniel did not have another competition until Karlstad on the 22nd. Throughout this period, the general pattern was for Daniel to lift on two consecutive days (normally after a morning throwing session), then have an easier day or even two days, then compete. To maintain this pattern, we treated June 18th as a competition day, with a morning wakeup call and an afternoon slam session where he took several throws at maximum effort. At this slam session, he threw 72.04m in good conditions.

We then restarted our pattern, with two days of lifting, a day of rest, and then the meeting at Karlstad.

Daniel Ståhl Program 12 Strength # 2	30/05-27/06 2021
SESSION 1	**SESSION 2**
19-Jun	
Cardio 60min (plus video/drills, few throws)	**Warm up:** Bike 5-10min
	Olympic Warmup: Sit Clean 3,2,1x100,120,140 or Snatch 3,2,1x70,80,90

	Lifting:
	Back Squats
	     3x5x62.5-72.5% = 200,215,230 or
	Front Squats
	     3x5x62.5-72.5% = 140,150,160

	Bench Press
	     3x5x67.5-77.5% = 145,155,165 or
	Incline D.P.
	     3x5x67.5-77.5% = 53.5,58.5,63.5

	Bent Over Row 3x8-10 or Lat Pull 3x8-10
	Leg Curl 3x10-12
	ABS & STABS: Upper, lower, rotation 3 sets each, DO IT!
20-Jun	
Warm up: Jog 5-10min	**Warm up:** Bike 5-10min

Hurdle walk or Running School: 5-10 hurdles, 5-10 ex/1-2x20-30mx5-10 ex.	**Lifting:**
	Push Press
	     3x5x67.5-77.5% = 140,150,160 or
	Press B. Neck
	     3x5x67.5-77.5% = 90,95,100

Fitness Warmup: Tommy Routine	**Sumo DL**
	     3x5x62.5-72.5% = 250,265,280 or
	Snatch Pull/Box
	     3x5x62.5-72.5% = 170,180,190

Throwing Discus: 2.0kg, 5 stand, 5-10 walks, 10 fulls NR, 10-15 fulls R (routine 60-65m)	Reverse Fly 3x8-10
Stretch: (Back, butt, hamstring, groin, hip flexor, chest)	Adduction 3x12-15
NO FOULS	**ABS & STABS:** Upper, lower, rotation 3 sets each, DO IT!
21-Jun	
REST	**REST**

22-Jun	
REST	**Warm up:** Jog 5-10min
(wake-up call Daniel Ståhl way, cardio, drills, video)	**Throwing Discus:** 2.0kg, Your warmup before the meet, D.S. own routine
	Stretch: (Back, butt, hamstring, groin, hip flexor, chest)

June 19

We did not throw in the morning, as Daniel needed time to recover from the previous day's slam session. We went back to 3x5 at 62.5-72.5% on squats and 3x5 at 67.5-77.5% on bench press in our afternoon lift.

June 20

This was a normal day of training with a throwing session in the morning and a 3x5 lifting session in the afternoon at the regular intensity. Notice we once again arranged Daniel's lifting schedule so he could do sumo deadlift two days before a competition.

June 21

This was a day of total rest and of travel to Karlstad.

June 22

Daniel performed well in rainy conditions in Karlstad. He had four legal attempts, all over 65 meters, with a best of 67.64m. Throwing well in lousy weather is another of Daniel's strengths. When the conditions are terrible with a tailwind and rain, he is hard to beat.

Daniel Ståhl Program 12 Strength # 2	30/05-27/06 2021
SESSION 1	**SESSION 2**
23-Jun	
Cardio 60min (plus video/drills, few throws)	**Warm up:** Bike 5-10min
	Olympic Warmup: Sit Clean 3,2,1x100,120,140 or Snatch 3,2,1x70,80,90

	Lifting:
	Back Squats
	    5,4,3x70-80% = 225,240,255+ or
	Front Squats
	    5,4,3x70-80% = 155,165,175+

	Bench Press
	    5,4,3x75-85% = 160,170,180+ or
	Incline D.P.
	    5,4,3x75-85% = 58.5,63.5,68.5+

	Bent Over Row 3x8-10 or Lat Pull 3x8-10
	Leg Curl 3x10-12
	ABS & STABS: Upper, lower, rotation 3 sets each, DO IT!
24-Jun	
Warm up: Jog 5-10min	**Warm up:** Bike 5-10min

Hurdle walk or Running School: 5-10 hurdles, 5-10 ex/1-2x20-30mx5-10 ex.	**Lifting:**
	Push Press
	    5,4,3x75-85% = 155,165,175 or
	Press B. Neck
	    4,3x75-85% = 100,105,110

Fitness Warmup: Tommy Routine	**Sumo DL**
	    5,4,3x70-80% = 270,285,300 or
	Snatch Pull/Box
	    5,4,3x70-80% = 180,190,200

Throwing Discus: 2.0kg, 5 stand, 5-10 walks, 10 fulls NR, 10-15 fulls R (routine 60-65m)	Reverse Fly 3x8-10
Stretch: (Back, butt, hamstring, groin, hip flexor, chest)	Adduction 3x12-15
NO FOULS	**ABS & STABS:** Upper, lower, rotation 3 sets each, DO IT!
25-Jun	
Cardio 60 min	**REST**

26-Jun	
REST	**Warm up:** Jog 5-10min
(wake-up call Daniel Ståhl way, cardio, drills, video)	**Throwing Discus:** 2.0kg, Your warmup before the meet, D.S. own routine
	Stretch: (Back, butt, hamstring, groin, hip flexor, chest)
27-Jun	
REST	Cardio 60min

June 23

After an easy morning, Daniel returned to lifting in the afternoon so we could maintain our pattern of lifting twice between competitions. Ideally, the day after a competition would be mostly rest, but I felt it was more important to stick to our rhythm of training at this time. These are the decisions coaches must make, and there would be more tough ones to come.

He did 5-4-3 in the weight room on this day at 75-85% for bench press and 70-80% for squats, which was also not ideal on the day following a competition, but he had already done his 3x5 sessions leading up to Karlstad, and to maintain his confidence and feeling, we needed to get back to 5-4-3 with the set of 3 being pretty heavy.

June 24

Here, we were back to our normal routine of throwing in the morning and lifting in the afternoon. Again, he did 5-4-3 at 75-85% with push press and 70-80% with sumo deadlift to get him feeling good for Kuortane.

June 25

Daniel did his morning walk, then traveled to Finland.

June 26

In the morning, Daniel took a walk for his usual wakeup call. That evening, he showed great spirit while battling the young phenom Kristjan Čeh. Daniel threw twice over 70-meters, including 70.55m in round six, to take the win. It made me extremely happy that he could beat Kristjan in Kristjan's best meet ever to that point and to win on his last throw. Kristjan's best on this day was 70.35m, an indication of the monster he was to become.

June 27

Daniel traveled back to Sweden and then did a cardio workout in the afternoon.

Daniel Ståhl Program 13 Strength # 3	28/06-13/07 2021
SESSION 1	**SESSION 2**
28-Jun	
Warm up: Jog 5-10min	**Warm up:** Bike 5-10min
Hurdle walk or Running School: 5-10 hurdles, 5-10 ex/1-2x20-30mx5-10 ex.	**Olympic Warmup:** Sit Clean 3,2,1x100,120,140 or Snatch 3,2,1x70,80,90
Fitness Warmup: Tommy Routine	**Lifting:** **Back Squats** 5,4,3x70-80% = 225,240,255+
Throwing Discus: 2.0kg, 5 stand, 5-10 walks, 5-10 fulls NR, 10-15 fulls R (routine 60-65m)	**Bench Press** 5,4,3x75-85% = 160,170,180+
Stretch: (Back, butt, hamstring, groin, hip flexor, chest)	Bent Over Row 3x8-10 or Lat Pull 3x8-10
NO FOULS	Leg Curl 3x10-12
	ABS & STABS: Upper, lower, rotation 3 sets each, DO IT!

29-Jun	
Warm up: Jog 5-10min	**Warm up:** Bike 5-10min

Hurdle walk or Running School: 5-10 hurdles, 5-10 ex/1-2x20-30mx5-10 ex.	**Lifting:**
	Push Press
	    3x5x67.5-77.5% = 140,150,160 or
	Press B. Neck
	    3x5x67.5-77.5% = 90,95,100

Fitness Warmup: Tommy Routine	**Sumo DL** 3x5x62.5-72.5% = 250,265,280
Throwing Discus: 2.0kg, Goal during Swedish Cup: 6 valid throws with a thought of 65m	Reverse Fly 3x8-10
Stretch: (Back, butt, hamstring, groin, hip flexor, chest)	Adduction 3x12-15
NO FOULS	**ABS & STABS:** Upper, lower, rotation 3 sets each, DO IT!
30-Jun	
REST	**REST**

June 28

On this day we did our normal two training sessions. As you can see, Daniel did a 5-4-3 lifting session for the second time in a row with 70-80% on squats and 75-85% on bench press, which goes against our normal pattern of alternating sessions of 5-4-3 and 3x5. We changed the pattern in this instance because he did not lift on the 25th, 26th, or 27th. After so much rest, this was an ideal day to sneak in a heavier session.

We then drove to Halmstad, where Daniel and Simon would compete the next day, representing their clubs in the Swedish Cup. It was certainly not ideal to be competing on this day with the Oslo Diamond League meeting coming shortly after, but these are the times when coaches earn their money.

June 29

I decided we would treat the Swedish Cup as a training session and told Daniel I wanted to see 6 legal throws in the 65-meter range. For him, that meant smooth, easy attempts at less than maximum effort. I hoped by taking this approach, we could avoid draining his energy. He is often exhausted after meetings, and with Oslo coming up so soon, he would not have his normal recovery time.

The results of this "experiment" were good. He produced 5 legal throws, 3 over 68-meters. That was fun, but now we had to face the most treacherous period of his schedule.

I had Daniel lift after the Swedish Cup meet before we left Halmstad. This was absolutely not ideal, but circumstances required it. This way, he could keep his training rhythm and get in his sumo deadlifts two days before Oslo.

June 30

This was a day of rest and a five-hour drive to Oslo.

Daniel Ståhl Program 13 Strength # 3	28/06-13/07 2021
SESSION 1	**SESSION 2**
1-Jul	
REST	**Warm up:** Jog 5-10min
(wake-up call Daniel Ståhl way, cardio, drills, video)	**Throwing Discus:** 2.0kg, Your warmup before the meet, D.S. own routine
	Stretch: (Back, butt, hamstring, groin, hip flexor, chest)

2-Jul	
Cardio 60min (plus video/drills, few throws)	**Warm up:** Bike 5-10min
	Olympic Warmup: Sit Clean 3,2,1x100,120,140 or Snatch 3,2,1x70,80,90
	Lifting: **Back Squats** 3x5x62.5-72.5% = 200,215,230

	Bench Press
	    3x5x67.5-77.5% = 145,155,165 or
	Incline D.P.
	    3x5x67.5-77.5% = 53.5,58.5,63.5

	Sumo DL 3x5x62.5-72.5% = 250,265,280
	Bent Over Row 3x8-10 or Lat Pull 3x8-10
	Leg Curl 3x10-12
	ABS & STABS: Upper, lower, rotation 3 sets each, DO IT!
3-Jul	
REST	REST

July 1

After a morning wake up call, Daniel competed in the Oslo Diamond League meeting. His technique was not perfect on this day, but he managed 6 legal throws, including the 4 farthest of the competition. His best was 68.65m, and he also threw 65.72m in the bullshit "final," which tied Kristjan Čeh. You may remember the Diamond League that year used a system where the top 3 throwers after 5 rounds each received a 6th attempt, and the winner of the competition was determined by the results of that final attempt regardless of how far anyone had thrown during the first 5 rounds. An athlete could literally break the world record during an early round but still lose the competition if they threw poorly on their 6th attempt! On this night, Daniel was credited with the win because the tiebreaker was who had the farthest throw in the regular competition.

July 2

We could not take a day of rest after Oslo, as the Stockholm Diamond League meeting was only three days away. Here, we had to improvise to stay as close to our normal rhythm as possible. On the drive back from Oslo, we stopped at Karlstad for a short throwing session. We had a fun time, met some local throwers, and were able to stop for lunch in Simon's hometown. We also lifted while in Karlstad and did the "combo" workout you can see on the chart, which included our regularly scheduled 3x5 at 62.5-72.5% in squats and 67.5-77.5% in bench, and also 3x5 at 62.5-72.5% in sumo deadlift to get Daniel ready for Stockholm.

To some, it may seem crazy to cram in a throwing and lifting session on the drive back from Oslo. Why not just take a couple of days off and be fresh for the Stockholm meet?

The problem is if an athlete starts skipping sessions when it is not convenient to do them, he will very likely lose the sense of comfort and confidence which comes from maintaining a consistent rhythm in training. I see this all the time with athletes who travel to Europe to compete for a few weeks in the summer. It is not easy to find places to lift weights when you are on the road, and many athletes give up trying. They lift sporadically or maybe even go two or three weeks without touching a weight. They hope that because they have lifted hard all year, they will not suffer from missing a few workouts.

And they are right in the sense that the body can retain strength for two or three weeks. It is the loss of routine which costs them.

I am not saying it is easy to maintain a normal training rhythm while traveling and competing. Over the years, I have spent many, many hours on the phone trying to arrange access to lifting gyms or throwing fields so my athletes could take their normal sessions no matter where they were traveling. During the ten years I trained Gerd Kanter, he and I worked together to arrange probably 60 lifting or throwing sessions each year while he was on the road. Those are sessions he would have had to skip had we not been determined to find ways to make them happen. If we couldn't get meeting promoters to promise in advance that Gerd would have access to a stadium where he could throw or to a weight room where he could lift, he would arrange it with local throwers or coaches. It is actually not uncommon for the head guy in charge of a meeting to always say no, so it is often better to arrange sessions with the local guys.

Over the course of his career, Gerd probably took 600 sessions this way that he otherwise would have missed. Did those 600 sessions help him become the World and Olympic champion? I believe they did.

July 3

Because we took the time to train on the way back from Oslo, we were able to take a rest day prior to competing in the Stockholm Diamond League meeting, which was the biggest meet for Daniel outside the Olympic Games that year. He felt very comfortable in Stockholm because he grew up there, and he always got excited about this meeting.

Daniel Ståhl Program 13 Strength # 3	28/06-13/07 2021
SESSION 1	**SESSION 2**
4-Jul	
REST	**Warm up:** Jog 5-10min
(wake-up call Daniel Ståhl way, cardio, drills, video)	**Throwing Discus:** 2.0kg, Your warmup before the meet, D.S. own routine
	Stretch: (Back, butt, hamstring, groin, hip flexor, chest)
	Warm up: Bike 5-10mi
	Lifting: **Back Squats** 　　3x5x62.5-72.5% = 200,215,230 **Bench Press** 　　3x5x67.5-77.5% = 145,155,165　or **Incline D.P.** 　　3x5x67.5-77.5% = 53.5,58.5,63.5
	Bent Over Row　3x8-10 or Lat Pull　　　　3x8-10
	Leg Curl　　　　3x10-12
	ABS & STABS: Upper, lower, rotation 3 sets each, DO IT!
5-Jul	
REST	REST
6-Jul	
REST	**Warm up:** Jog 5-10min
(wake-up call Daniel Ståhl way, cardio, drills, video)	**Throwing Discus:** 2.0kg, Your warmup before the meet, D.S. own routine
	Stretch: (Back, butt, hamstring, groin, hip flexor, chest)
7-Jul	
REST	REST
8-Jul	
REST	Cardio 60min

July 4

We did our normal morning wakeup call, and then in the evening, Daniel competed in Stockholm and performed very well. He had 3 fouls, but his legal throws were 67.33m, 68.64m, and 68.23m. Despite the hectic schedule, this was his fourth competition in a row over 68-meters, which gave him a lot of confidence looking ahead to the Games.

As you can see, we did a lifting session that same night. Again, not an ideal situation, but doing this lift after the competition allowed him to use the following day to rest and travel to Hungary, where he would compete on July 6th.

In this lifting session, Daniel did squats for 3x5 at 62.5-72.5% and bench for 3x5 at 67.5-77.5%. This was a change from our routine of alternating 3x5 sessions with 5-4-3 sessions, but I made the adjustment because I was afraid he was running out of gas and a heavier 5-4-3 session might be too much for him. You may also notice that I did not have Daniel do sumo deadlift in this workout, even though he had a meeting coming up in two days.

With competitions scheduled on June 29, July 1,4,6, and 10, we had no choice but to alter our usual approach. The reason for this crazy schedule was Covid, which caused some organizers to shuffle the dates of their meetings. Both the Swedish Cup and the Oslo Diamond League meetings were rescheduled due to Covid, and both ended up being crammed into this period.

Why not just skip one or two of these competitions?

Well, the Diamond League meetings are important because they give throwers a chance to make a little money. I asked Daniel and Simon if they wanted to skip the Swedish Cup, but it was important to them to represent their clubs. And we had given our word that we would compete in Hungary, and I always wanted our word to mean something. Besides, the man running the meeting in Hungary was a good guy, and we wanted to treat him right and show respect for his work.

So, I would alter our plan and do our best to get us through this crazy period.

July 5

This was a day of rest and travel to Hungary for the Gyulai István Memorial meeting.

July 6

Daniel did his usual wakeup call and then competed in the Gyulai István Memorial, which he won with a best throw of 67.71m. It was very hot with no wind, so I was happy with his distance and even happier that he made it through without being injured.

Now, he only had one more meeting before we departed for Tokyo.

July 7

This was a day of rest and travel.

July 8

Another day of rest with only a session of cardio in the afternoon.

Daniel Ståhl Program 13 Strength # 3	28/06-13/07 2021
SESSION 1	**SESSION 2**
9-Jul	
Warm up: Jog 5-10min	**Warm up:** Bike 5-10min
Hurdle walk or Running School: 5-10 hurdles, 5-10 ex/1-2x20-30mx5-10 ex.	**Olympic Warmup:** Sit Clean 3,2,1x100,120,140 or Snatch 3,2,1x70,80,90
Fitness Warmup: Tommy Routine	**Lifting:** **Back Squats** 5,4,3x70-80% = 225,240,255
Throwing Discus: 2.0kg, 5 stand, 5-10 walks, 5-10 fulls NR, 10-15 fulls R (routine 60-65m)	**Bench Press** 5,4,3x75-85% = 160,170,180
Stretch: (Back, butt, hamstring, groin, hip flexor, chest)	Bent Over Row 3x8-10 or Lat Pull 3x8-10
NO FOULS	Leg Curl 3x10-12
	ABS & STABS: Upper, lower, rotation 3 sets each, DO IT!
10-Jul	
REST	**Warm up:** Jog 5-10min
	Throwing Discus: 2.0kg, Your warmup before the meet, D.S. own routine
	Stretch: (Back, butt, hamstring, groin, hip flexor, chest)
11-Jul	
Cardio 60min (plus video/drills, few throws)	**Warm up:** Bike 5-10min
	Lifting: **Push Press** 5,4,3x75-85% = 155,165,175
	Sumo DL 5,4,3x70-80% = 270,285,300
	Reverse Fly 3x8-10
	Adduction 3x12-15
	ABS & STABS: Upper, lower, rotation 3 sets each, DO IT!
12-Jul	
REST	**REST**
13-Jul	
REST	**Cardio 60min**

July 9

We did an easy throwing session in the morning and lifting in the afternoon with 5-4-3 at 70-80% on squats and 75-85% on bench press.

July 10

We rested in the morning instead of doing the usual wake-up call, then in the evening, Daniel competed in the Bottnaryd throwers meeting, his final competition before the Olympic Games. I decided we would approach this meeting the same as we had the Swedish Cup--as a workout. I wanted to see Daniel take 6 attempts at submaximal effort and get through it feeling healthy.

He ended up throwing a world-leading distance of 71.40m, probably because he felt so relaxed after making it through the grind of the previous month. He had a lot of fun during the competition, and when he has fun, he usually throws very well.

July 11

In the morning, Daniel did a cardio workout, and then in the afternoon, we got in one final lifting session before departing for our training camp in Fukuoka on the 12th. His lifts were 5-4-3 at 70-80% in sumo deadlift and 75-85% in push press.

Success

The goal during this phase was to allow Daniel to throw far while also staying strong. If we pulled the plug on hard training too early, it would have diminished his chances to be at his best in Tokyo. On the other hand, if we were not careful, he might have become exhausted and even injured with little time to recover before our final preparations for the Games.

Daniel's performance during this phase proved we had found the right balance. He not only won every meet he entered, but he finished the busiest part of our schedule with his best throw of the summer.

After the Bottnaryd meeting, he told me he was the happiest man on Earth. "I have the world-leading throw," he said, "and now we go to Fukuoka and relax."

Second Blue Period - Fukuoka, July 14-31, 2021

The final training days leading up to an Olympics can be a treacherous time. The stresses of travel and of adapting to an unfamiliar environment, along with the pressure of wanting to perform well under the Olympic spotlight, can make it difficult for athletes and even coaches to stay in balance mentally and physically.

Daniel, Simon, and Fanny all had success in Tokyo, and an important reason why was because we managed the two weeks prior to the Games in a way that let everyone stay calm, happy, and focused on the simple act of throwing a shot put or discus.

This did not happen by accident. I learned through many years of experience the conditions necessary to produce an optimum performance at an Olympics, and with the help of the Swedish Athletic Federation, the Swedish Olympic Committee and our support staff, we were able to create such conditions.

The first issue we had to deal with was the question of when to arrive in Japan. Adaptation to the seven-hour time change from Sweden to Tokyo was a key consideration. Theoretically, there are two ways to manage a situation like this. One is to wait until the day before a competition to fly in. It takes a day or so for jet lag to hit, and sometimes, it is possible to perform well before feeling the effects. This would not have worked for us, however, as the qualification round and the finals were on different days, so even if we performed well in qualification, we would have been in big trouble for the final. Also, Covid protocols made traveling more complicated than ever, and so planning to arrive the day before qualification would have been very risky. Any delay in traveling would put the athletes through enormous stress, and our goal in the days leading up to the Games was to create less stress, not more.

The other method of helping athletes adapt to a significant time change is to provide at least one day of adaptation for each hour of time difference.

This is the method I follow, and in this case, it meant we could arrive in Japan no later than July 23rd, as the men's discus qualification was scheduled for the 30th.

I have seen coaches try to fudge this one-day-per-hour rule, and I do not recommend it. Going into the 2007 World Championships in Osaka, Gerd Kanter lost to Virgilijus Alekna forty-four of the forty-five times they faced each other. We arrived in Japan two weeks before the Worlds, but for some reason, Virgilijus arrived much later and gave himself only four days to adapt. He was still in his prime then and had a season's best of 71.56m, but in Osaka, he threw only 65.24m and finished fourth. Gerd won with 68.94m.

That experience reinforced in me the need to always provide my athletes with the opportunity to acclimate to a change in time zone.

Another important factor for us in formulating our travel plans was my determination to maintain our normal pattern of training.

As I have described, we did our best every year, from the first sessions in October to the final competitions in September, to maintain a specific rhythm in our practice schedule. That basic rhythm usually consisted of two sessions on Monday, two on Tuesday, and one on Wednesday. We repeated that pattern from Thursday through Saturday, then took Sunday off. This plan could be altered slightly depending on the needs of each individual athlete, and we obviously had to adjust during the competitive season as we could not dictate the days on which meets occurred, but even then, we tried to stick to our training pattern as closely as possible.

Maintaining a consistent rhythm in training provided the athlete with a sense of physical and mental well-being, and the last thing I ever wanted to do was to disrupt this feeling in the days before an important competition such as an Olympic Games or World Championships.

With that in mind, we decided to travel to our training camp in Fukuoka on July 16th. This would allow us a day of travel and then a full two weeks of training in our normal rhythm prior to the men's discus and women's shot put qualification. A couple of weeks prior to our departure, however, we found out that our flight had been canceled.

We were instead offered a choice between traveling on the 17th or leaving several days earlier than planned and flying to Japan on the 12th. Even though it meant leaving the comforts of our training base in Växjö and spending extra days under the strict Covid protocols and unfamiliar conditions we were likely to face in Japan, we chose to take the earlier flight because doing so guaranteed that we could fit in two full weeks of rhythmical training before the Games.

And thanks to the Swedish Olympic Committee, we were able to book business class seats--an important consideration for big guys like Simon and Daniel--on a charter flight on the 12th, which flew directly to Fukuoka.

The flight gave me time to reflect on all we had been through over the summer. In some ways, I felt like the happiest coach on Earth when we got on the plane because up to that point, the season had gone so well. We had not missed a single training session due to Covid. Daniel, Simon, and Fanny had all survived the difficult stretch in June and July, where our schedule was crammed with traveling and competing. All three would arrive in Japan strong, healthy, and in good spirits.

On that flight, I was also thinking about my sister, Aðalbjörg Hafsteinsdóttir. Growing up in Selfoss, we were a big family, with few material possessions. My mother made all our clothes, and we never went out to eat. The first time I went with my parents to a restaurant in our town, I was forty-six years old!

But we had sports and the Ölfusá River, where we would go fishing, and the flat-topped mountain called Ingólfsfjall, where we would hide behind the rocks, shoot each other with cap pistols, and imagine we were American cowboys.

And we had each other. I was the youngest, and all my siblings played a part in making my childhood wonderful.

But twelve days before the flight to Fukuoka, I found out my sister had stage 4 cancer.

I thought about her a lot while I was in Japan, and it helped me to keep my perspective and remember to sleep and eat and not let the possibilities overwhelm me, which is something I have struggled with during my career.

On more than one occasion, I have been hospitalized from exhaustion. In 2016, I had two episodes in one day where my heart rate went crazy, and I thought I was going to die. The doctor who attended to me said I would be okay but asked when was the last time I took a day of rest. I checked my calendar and saw I had worked sixty-six days in a row.

During the spring of 2021, I started to fall into the same trap. As defending World Champion, Daniel was the favorite to take the gold medal in Tokyo, but as I have described, there was a time during the spring when I was not happy with the way he was throwing, and I could not figure out how to help him correct it. I started waking up in the middle of the night and getting out of bed to watch video, searching for the answer that could unlock his potential.

I worried we might be blowing an opportunity to do amazing things in 2021, and I knew I would not be able to forgive myself if we did.

I began to get very negative and frustrated, and that is when my wife Anna said, "Enough."

She made me calm down and realize I can only do what I can do. My athletes are human, and I am human, and we would do our best and see what would happen. Finding out about my sister's illness also reminded me that sports are not life and no matter how my athletes performed at the Games, life, with all its ups and downs, would continue.

This was my frame of mind as we traveled to Fukuoka.

I was also very thankful because we would have our support staff with us during the training camp. Tommy Eriksson (physical therapist), Henrik Wagner (massage therapist), Henrik Gustafsson (mental coach), and Linda Bakkman (nutritionist) would all be there. They would help very much to make things feel normal.

And I want to make an important point here. Establishing a "normal," comfortable feeling should be the goal at a training camp like the one we had in Fukuoka.

The Olympics are obviously the most important competition in the career of a thrower, so it is human nature to want to make the final training sessions leading up to them the "best ever" and to think that by doing so you can ensure your athlete will have their best performance ever. But this is a mistake.

The truth is there is very little you can do in the two weeks prior to the Games to cause an athlete to have the performance of his or her lifetime. It is the years of training and competing prior to the Olympics which determine their chances of medaling.

The night before the 2008 Olympic final, my friend Raul Rebane invited me to join him for dinner to celebrate Gerd winning the gold. This may sound funny because Gerd had not yet won the gold, but Raul pointed out that Gerd's average in his top ten meets for the 2008 season was 68.80m. All he had to do was have an "average" day, make an "average" throw in the final, and he would win.

And that is what happened. In the final, Gerd threw 68.82m and took the gold medal. I asked him afterward if the 68.82m felt like a good throw. He said no, only "average."

But it was the many years of hard work leading up to Beijing that made him the Olympic champion, not anything special we did during our final days of preparation.

And it would be the same for Daniel, Fanny, and Simon in Tokyo. I hoped Daniel, the defending World Champion, would win the gold medal. I hoped Simon, as an up-and-coming contender, would finish in the top five or six and set himself up to compete for a medal in Paris in 2024. I hoped Fanny, who had never advanced to the final of an outdoor global championships, would do so in Tokyo and also end up in the top eight.

Those would be special achievements, yes, but to accomplish these things, all each of them had to do was to have a normal day.

Daniel's average best throw in his top ten meets in 2021 prior to the Olympics was 69.06m. In Tokyo, this would likely get him the gold medal. Simon's top-ten average was 66.13m, which would very likely place him in the top six at the Games. Fanny's top-ten average was 18.99m, a distance which would get her into the Tokyo final and probably the top eight.

So, there was no need to try to make our time in Fukuoka the "greatest training camp ever." Which is good, because it wasn't. Daniel's best throw during those two weeks was 69.40m. Simon's was 66.60m. Fanny had one throw of 19.45m, but on most days, her best throws were around 19 meters. And all three missed on a lot of throws during those two weeks, just like in "normal" training sessions. Knowing we did not have to be perfect, that all Fanny, Simon, and Daniel had to do was to prepare to throw an average throw in the Games, kept me from getting stressed and from passing stress onto them.

I actually did very little technical coaching in Fukuoka. One day, Fanny got mad at me because she thought I was ignoring her. She was throwing at the same time as the discus guys, and because I was saying so little, she thought I was only paying attention to them. But I was just following my plan.

A training camp before a major championship is not the time to make technical changes. In Fukuoka, I just wanted to reinforce the things which had made Daniel, Simon, and Fanny throw far all summer. On Daniel's workout plan, you will see that I often wrote "focus on the packet" and "push with the right leg."

"The packet" refers to technical points we worked on earlier regarding Daniel's timing as he finished his swing and shifted into the entry phase of the throw. His right arm and the left shoulder needed to be in a specific position when his right foot came off the ground. Rather than dividing this position into different components ("left shoulder here" "right arm with the discus here" "right foot comes up here") I just started referring to all these cues together as "the packet."

"Push with the right leg" was a reminder not to reverse too early, but to stay on the ground and generate power with his right leg until the discus left his hand.

These were cues Daniel had heard from me many times throughout the summer. In Fukuoka, they helped him maintain a good feel for his technique and kept him from thinking too much.

I also spoke to our support team every day and always reminded them to do no more or no less than they would if we were training back in Växjö. With a lot of time on our hands in Fukuoka, it would be easy for them to schedule extra sessions with the athletes, but it was important to avoid this so as not to create the feeling that we had to do more than usual in the days leading up to the Games in order to have a good performance.

So, Tommy worked on their backs and other body parts the usual amount, and Henrik G. spoke with them every third day or so. Henrik W. kept his normal massage appointments with them. Because of the heat, Linda checked their hydration levels daily, and at one point, we had to adjust

Daniel's intake of fluids, but she was careful not to make a big deal of it. We wanted to avoid creating any feelings of drama.

There was one more aspect of our environment in Fukuoka which I think helped our group to perform well in the Games, and that is the bond that grew between Simon, Fanny, and Daniel. They had always gotten along well, but their friendship deepened as the Olympics approached. Simon and Daniel, for example, chose to room together in Japan even though they could each have had their own space.

It may seem obvious that athletes who train together every day should become friends, but that is not always the case. It is not unusual for the best throwers to be hyper-competitive and hyper-focused. Once guys like Gerd and Joachim Olsen figured out what it took to get to the top, they were not going to let anyone, or anything interfere with their journey. When I was working with Joachim, we were meant to do a lifting session in a training hall in Denmark one day, but there was a soccer match in a nearby stadium, and for security purposes the police had closed the hall. Joachim was not going to miss his workout, so he simply refused to leave until they unlocked the door for us, which caused quite a fuss. A "normal" person would have accepted they would not be able to do their session that day and left without causing trouble. But top athletes are usually not "normal," and their intense nature can cause a divide between them and other members of a training group.

But Daniel has a very different personality. He fought his way to the top like Gerd did, but still likes to get along with everyone. So even though he was the best discus thrower in the world, it was easy for the others to be friends with Daniel, and all three of my throwers benefited from this bond as we prepared for the Games.

So now I will go through the training sessions we did in Fukuoka day by day.

Daniel Ståhl Prog 14 Speed & Power #2	**14/07-31/07 2021**
SESSION 1	**SESSION 2**
14-Jul	
Warm up: Jog 5-10min	**Warm up:** Bike 5-10min
Hurdle walk: 5-10 hurdles, 5-10 ex + Tommy routine	**Olympic Warmup:** Sit Clean 3,2,1x100,120,140 or Snatch 3,2,1x70,80,90
Throwing Discus: 2.0kg, 5 Stand NR, 5 Fulls NR, 10-15 Fulls R, submax 90-95% NO FOULS	**Lifting:** **Back Squats Warmup: 3x3-5x110,150,190** 5,4,3x65-75% = 210,225,240
Stretch: (Back, butt, hamstring, groin, hip flexor, chest)	**Bench Press Warmup: 3x3-5x100,120,140** 5,4,3x75-82.5% = 162.5,170,177.5
YOU SHOULD THROW ROUTINE THROWS WITH REVERSE, ALL THE SAME	Bent Over Row 3x8-10 or Lat Pull 3x8-10
FOCUS ON THE PACKET, PUSH WITH RIGHT LEG	Leg Curl 3x10-12
	ABS & STABS: Upper, lower, rotation 3 sets each, DO IT!

July 14

We flew to Fukuoka from Copenhagen on June 12th and arrived around 9:00 a.m. local time on the 13th. Because of the Covid protocols, it took five hours from when we landed to when we finally made it to the hotel.

The Japanese people are very pleasant, but the Covid procedures were strict. We had to download an app on which we registered our health every day. We also had to do a daily PCR test.

On our first day in Fukuoka, we could only leave the hotel to go to training. After that, we were allowed to walk on a nearby beach each day between the hours of 6:00-9:00 a.m. and 4:00-7:00 p.m. Otherwise, we were supposed to be on our floor in the hotel or in the large team room set up for Swedish athletes.

We were allowed to eat together, but each table was segmented into five places by plastic dividers. The serving sizes were quite small compared to what an American or European is used to, but the food was served buffet style, and the dining area was open all the time, so you could eat as much as you wanted.

When new groups of Swedish athletes arrived, they were kept in a kind of quarantine for three days. We could not eat with them or hang out with them. Each group was allowed to train right away, but for three days, they had to be transported separately from those of us who arrived earlier.

When we showed up at the stadium for our first throwing session on the 14th, we were told the only ones allowed to practice there were the soccer players. As always, the Japanese staff was very nice about the situation, but they are very strict about following orders, so our boss--the head of the Swedish team--had to call their boss to get things straightened out.

This kind of thing is not uncommon when you travel. Once, when we did a training camp in Spain, we were told, "No training on Sundays." Of course, during a training camp, we have to train on Sundays, and after one or two days, we got that worked out.

This was another reason I wanted us to arrive in Japan as early as possible--to have time to work through any misunderstandings.

So, after about thirty minutes, we were directed to the hammer field. After that first session, we trained either in the main stadium or on the throwing field, and both facilities were just fine.

The throwing session on the 14th took place in tough conditions. It was something like 93 degrees Fahrenheit, with 85-90 percent humidity. But we were there to get acclimated, so we began the process with an easy session.

You can see I made a note on his workout telling Daniel to throw "routine throws with reverse, all the same." I knew he would be tired on this day, but I wanted to establish right away our focus on consistency. And even when we threw harder later in the camp, we were never looking for PBs or world records, just consistent, repeatable technique.

You will also see on this day the cues I mentioned earlier, "focus on the packet" and "push with the right leg."

In terms of lifting, Daniel did only his favorite exercises (back squat, bench press, push press, sumo deadlift) during the Fukuoka camp. This was according to our plan to help him feel happy and comfortable in the days leading up to the Games.

It was important to keep the intensity of lifting and throwing low after making such a long trip, and our goal those first few days was to set up the training rhythm while working through jet lag.

There is one unusual aspect to the lifting workouts in Fukuoka that I need to explain. You will notice I have included warmup sets with specific weights for each of the main lifts. This is not something I would normally do during other parts of the season. During the yellow phases, for example, Daniel might perform one brief warmup set at a weight of his choosing then go right into the prescribed sets and reps.

It may seem crazy to add extra warmup sets at a time when we were meant to taper by lowering volume in his lifts, but because Daniel was so big I always worried that if we reduced the volume too much, he would start to feel sloppy, which would have a negative effect on his confidence and his feeling for the throw. And remember, unlike when I reduced his load in May, we no longer had time to get him back on track if he lost his feel.

It was crazy how much time I spent worrying about this in the weeks leading up to the Games, but I kept thinking about how Daniel had performed at the World Championships in Doha in 2019. After consistently throwing 69 meters or better that season, Daniel was the big favorite to take the gold medal at the Doha Worlds, and this pressure weighed heavy on him. As a result, he could not find his rhythm in the ring, but he won anyway because he was strong enough to throw 67.59m with terrible technique.

Daniel was also the favorite to win in Tokyo, which put even more pressure on him because the Olympics are a much bigger deal than the World Championships. It seemed reasonable to me that Daniel might once again have to win on strength, which he would not be able to do if he was feeling sluggish from the travel, the time difference, the heat, and the lack of volume in his lifting. I was determined to prepare him in a way that would allow him to rely on his biggest assets--his strength and power--in the Tokyo final, so I added the warmup sets to his main lifts hoping he would feel strong and ready to rock and roll even as we kept the volume and intensity of his work sets low.

In this I set training theory aside and went by feeling and by my understanding of how Daniel works, an understanding that came from training him for ten years.

Daniel Ståhl Prog 14 Speed & Power #2	14/07-31/07 2021
SESSION 1	**SESSION 2**
15-Jul	
Warm up: Jog 5-10min	**Warm up:** Bike 5-10min
Hurdle walk: 5-10 hurdles, 5-10 ex + Tommy routine	**Lifting:** **Push Press** Warmup: 3x3-5x100,120,140 5,4,3x72.5-80% = 150,157.5,165
Throwing Discus: 2.0kg, 5 Static NR, 5 Fulls NR & 10-15 Fulls R, submax 90-95% NO FOULS	**Sumo DL** Warmup: 3x3-5x140,180,220 5,4,3x62.5-70% = 250,265,280
Stretch: (Back, butt, hamstring, groin, hip flexor, chest)	Reverse Fly 3x8-10
15-20 WALKS BEFORE YOU START THROWING, FOCUS ON THE PACKET, PUSH WITH THE RIGHT LEG	Adduction 3x12-15
A LOT OF DRILLS AND VIDEO	**ABS & STABS:** Upper, lower, rotation 3 sets each, DO IT!
16-Jul	
REST	**REST**

17-Jul	
Warm up: Jog 5-10min	**Warm up:** Bike 5-10min
Hurdle walk: 5-10 hurdles, 5-10 ex + Tommy routine	**Olympic Warmup:** Sit Clean 3,2,1x100,120,140 or Snatch 3,2,1x70,80,90
Throwing Discus: 2.0kg, 5 Stand NR, 5 Fulls NR, 10-15 Fulls R, submax 90-95% NO FOULS	**Lifting:** **Back Squats** **Warmup: 3x3-5x110,150,190** 5,4,3x67.5-77.5% = 215,232.5,250
Stretch: (Back, butt, hamstring, groin, hip flexor, chest)	**Bench Press** **Warmup: 3x3-5x100,120,140** 5,4,3x77.5-85% = 167.5,175,182.5
YOU SHOULD THROW ROUTINE THROWS WITH A REVERSE, ALL THE SAME	Bent Over Row 3x8-10 or Lat Pull 3x8-10
FOCUS ON THE PACKET, PUSH WITH THE RIGHT LEG	Leg Curl 3x10-12
	ABS & STABS: Upper, lower, rotation 3 sets each, DO IT!
18-Jul	
Warm up: Jog 5-10min	**Warm up:** Bike 5-10min
Hurdle walk: 5-10 hurdles, 5-10 ex + Tommy routine	**Lifting:** **Push Press** **Warmup: 3x3-5x100,120,140** 5,4,3x75-82.5% = 155,162.5,170
Throwing Discus: 2.0kg, 5 Static NR, 5 Fulls NR & 10-15 Fulls R, submax 90-95% NO FOULS	**Sumo DL** **Warmup: 3x3-5x140,180,220** 5,4,3x65-72.5% = 260,275,290
Stretch: (Back, butt, hamstring, groin, hip flexor, chest)	Reverse Fly 3x8-10
15-20 WALKS BEFORE YOU START THROWING, FOCUS ON THE PACKET, PUSH WITH THE RIGHT LEG	Adduction 3x12-15
A LOT OF DRILLS AND VIDEO	**ABS & STABS:** Upper, lower, rotation 3 sets each, DO IT!
19-Jul	
REST	**REST**

July 15

The sessions on this day were pretty much the same as on the 14th: low intensity throwing and sets of 5-4-3 in the weight room at fairly low percentages.

July 16

This was a day of rest. During most of the year, Daniel would have a short mobility/stability/cardio session on the third day of a training week, but we dropped those sessions during the Fukuoka camp and gave him extra rest instead.

July 17

In the morning, we did another throwing session with fairly low intensity. You can see we stuck with sets of 5-4-3 on his lifts that afternoon, but we raised the intensity slightly on both back squats and bench presses.

July 18

Our sessions on this day were just like the previous ones we had done since arriving in Fukuoka. We kept focused on rhythmical throws in the morning and did 5-4-3 with pretty easy weights in the afternoon.

July 19

This was another day of rest.

Daniel Ståhl Prog 14 Speed & Power #2	14/07-31/07 2021
SESSION 1	**SESSION 2**
20-Jul	
Warm up: Jog 5-10min	**Warm up:** Bike 5-10min
Hurdle walk: 5-10 hurdles, 5-10 ex + Tommy routine	**Olympic Warmup:** Sit Clean 3,2,1x100,120,140 or Snatch 3,2,1x70,80,90
Throwing Discus: 2.0kg, 3-5 Stand NR, 6-12 Fulls R, submax-max 95-100% NO FOULS	**Lifting:** **Back Squats** Warmup: 3x3-5x110,150,190 3x3x72.5-82.5% = 235,250,265+
Stretch: (Back, butt, hamstring, groin, hip flexor, chest)	**Bench Press** Warmup: 3x3-5x100,120,140 3x3x80-87.5% = 172.5,180,187.5+
This is a slam session. Warm up as in a competition.	Bent Over Row 3x8-10 or Lat Pull 3x8-10
	Leg Curl 3x10-12
	ABS & STABS: Upper, lower, rotation 3 sets each, DO IT!
21-Jul	
Warm up: Jog 5-10min	**Warm up:** Bike 5-10min
Hurdle walk: 5-10 hurdles, 5-10 ex + Tommy routine	**Lifting:** **Push Press** Warmup: 3x3-5x100,120,140 3x3x77.5-85% = 160,167.5,175
Throwing Discus: 2.0kg, 5 Static NR, 5 Fulls NR & 10-15 Fulls R, submax 90-95% NO FOULS	**Sumo DL** Warmup: 3x3-5x140,180,220 3x3x67.5-75% = 270,285,300
Stretch: (Back, butt, hamstring, groin, hip flexor, chest)	Reverse Fly 3x8-10
15-20 WALKS BEFORE YOU START THROWING, FOCUS ON THE PACKET, PUSH WITH THE RIGHT LEG	Adduction 3x12-15
Lots of drills and video	**ABS & STABS:** Upper, lower, rotation 3 sets each, DO IT!
22-Jul	
REST	REST

23-Jul	
Warm up: Jog 5-10min	**Warm up:** Bike 5-10min
Hurdle walk: 5-10 hurdles, 5-10 ex + Tommy routine	**Olympic Warmup:** Sit Clean 3,2,1x100,120,140 or Snatch 3,2,1x70,80,90
Throwing Discus: 2.0kg, 3-5 Stand NR, 6-12 Fulls R, submax-max 95-100% NO FOULS	**Lifting:** **Back Squats** Warmup: 3x3-5x110,150,190 3x3x72.5-82.5% = 235,250,265+
Stretch: (Back, butt, hamstring, groin, hip flexor, chest)	**Bench Press** Warmup: 3x3-5x100,120,140 3x3x80-87.5% = 172.5,180,187.5+
This is a slam session. Warm up as in a competition.	Bent Over Row 3x8-10 or Lat Pull 3x8-10
	Leg Curl 3x10-12
	ABS & STABS: Upper, lower, rotation 3 sets each, DO IT!
24-Jul	
Warm up: Jog 5-10min	**Warm up:** Bike 5-10min
Hurdle walk: 5-10 hurdles, 5-10 ex + Tommy routine	**Lifting:** **Push Press** Warmup: 3x3-5x100,120,140 3x3x77.5-85% = 160,167.5,175
Throwing Discus: 2.0kg, 5 Static NR, 5 Fulls NR & 10-15 Fulls R, submax 90-95% NO FOULS	**Sumo DL** Warmup: 3x3-5x140,180,220 3x3x67.5-75% = 270,285,300
Stretch: (Back, butt, hamstring, groin, hip flexor, chest)	Reverse Fly 3x8-10
15-20 WALKS BEFORE YOU START THROWING, FOCUS ON THE PACKET, PUSH WITH THE RIGHT LEG	Adduction 3x12-15
Lots of drills and video	**ABS & STABS:** Upper, lower, rotation 3 sets each, DO IT!
25-Jul	
REST	**REST**

July 20

In the morning, we did our first slam session of the camp, and Daniel threw 69.40m. This showed he was adapting well to the heat and the time change. It was interesting to me that Daniel was responding exactly the way Gerd had during our training camp for the 2011 Worlds in Osaka. I put

Daniel on the same schedule we had devised for Gerd then, and both came to life during their first slam session.

In the weight room, we once again nudged up the intensity by around two percent, but we changed the sets and reps to 3x3 with a focus on moving the bar with speed. Our lifting sessions in Fukuoka were short, maybe 45-60 minutes, which left plenty of energy for the throwing ring.

July 21

In the morning, we did an easier throwing session, just focusing on rhythm and feel. Notice the volume of our throws during the Fukuoka camp was low, usually 6-15 full throws.

Remember, we were not in Fukuoka to get in shape. After a long year of training, these sessions were the cream on the cake.

In the afternoon lift, we stuck with 3x3 and once again added two percent to the intensity.

July 22

This was another day of rest.

July 23

We had another slam session in the morning and another 3x3 lifting session in the afternoon. Notice we did not raise the intensity from the last time he did back squats and bench presses. This was part of our effort to make Daniel feel strong and fit without burning too much energy on lifting.

July 24

In the morning, we did a technical throwing session, and in the afternoon, 3x3 on push press and sumo deadlift with the same weight as he used three days earlier on these lifts.

July 25

A day of rest.

Daniel Ståhl Prog 14 Speed & Power #2	14/07-31/07 2021
SESSION 1	**SESSION 2**
26-Jul	
Warm up: Jog 5-10min	**Warm up:** Bike 5-10min
Hurdle walk: 5-10 hurdles, 5-10 ex + Tommy routine	**Olympic Warmup:** Sit Clean 3,2,1x100,120,140 or Snatch 3,2,1x70,80,90
Throwing Discus: 2.0kg, 5 Static NR, 5 Fulls NR & 10-15 Fulls R, submax 90-95% NO FOULS	**Lifting:** **Back Squats** Warmup: 3x3-5x110,150,190 3x3x65-75% = 210,225,240
Stretch: (Back, butt, hamstring, groin, hip flexor, chest)	**Bench Press** Warmup: 3x3-5x100,120,140 3x3x75-82.5% = 162.5,170,177.5
15-20 WALKS BEFORE YOU START THROWING, FOCUS ON THE PACKET, PUSH WITH THE RIGHT LEG	Bent Over Row 3x8-10 or Lat Pull 3x8-10
Lots of drills and video	Leg Curl 3x10-12
	ABS & STABS: Upper, lower, rotation 3 sets each, DO IT!

27-Jul	
Warm up: Jog 5-10min	**Warm up:** Bike 5-10min
Hurdle walk: 5-10 hurdles, 5-10 ex + Tommy routine	**Lifting:** **Push Press** Warmup: 3x3-5x100,120,140 3x3x72.5-80% = 150,157.5,165
Throwing Discus: 2.0kg, 5 Stand NR, 5 Fulls NR, 10-15 Fulls R, submax 90-95% NO FOULS	**Sumo DL** Warmup: 3x3-5x140,180,220 3x3x62.5-70% = 250,265,280
Stretch: (Back, butt, hamstring, groin, hip flexor, chest)	Reverse Fly 3x8-10
YOU SHOULD THROW ROUTINE THROWS WITH REVERSE, ALL THE SAME	Adduction 3x12-15
FOCUS ON THE PACKET, PUSH WITH THE RIGHT LEG	**ABS & STABS:** Upper, lower, rotation 3 sets each, DO IT!

July 26 and 27

We did not need to see PBs in training at this point to know we were ready to perform well in Tokyo. In his final slam session prior to the 2005 World Championships, Gerd Kanter threw 61.98m. My friend Nick Sweeney the Irish discus thrower was there, and he told me not to worry. "The kid has been throwing damn good lately," he said. "He's going to do great in the competition."

Nick was right. Gerd threw 68.57m and got the silver medal.

Rather than the results from one training session or one competition, it is the athlete's overall body of work that shows if they are prepared.

So, we did not seek confirmation in these final sessions that Daniel was ready to throw well in the Games.

Our motto leading up to qualification was "How hard can it be?"

During the qualification round at the Olympics later that week, each athlete would be given two warmup throws. Then, they would take either one, two, or three throws in the competition, depending on whether they achieved the automatic qualifying mark. If each throw required the athlete to focus for one minute, then the qualification round would demand a maximum of five minutes of concentrated work. I try to give my athletes one thing to think about when they compete--one simple technical point. So, all they needed to do was focus on that point five times for one minute at a time.

How hard can it be?

What makes it hard is when you start thinking about how you had a lousy breakfast, or about the bad weather, or how you forgot your water bottle. Or, if you let yourself make the Olympic Games bigger than other competition and decide that you must press down hard on the gas pedal to get a big throw.

Our final meet before traveling to Japan took place in Bottnaryd, Sweden, in front of maybe three hundred spectators. In Tokyo, millions of people would be watching on television. But we were doing the exact same thing in both instances--throwing the shot put and the discus as far as possible by focusing on a single technical point one minute at a time.

How hard can it be?

On Monday the 26th and Tuesday the 27th, we held our final training sessions before the qualification round.

During our throwing sessions, Daniel, Fanny, and Simon worked on the "one thing" they were meant to focus on in the competition.

With Daniel, we focused on "the packet." Our goal was for him to maintain separation out of the back and into the middle of the circle. Essentially, we wanted to see the position he established in his swing--that really good separation--as he ran the ring. It is a position similar to the second step in the javelin approach.

When Ryan Crouser was asked to explain his world record throw in June of 2021, he spoke about the feeling of having his chest up and facing the direction of the throw for a long time as he began his sprint. That is another way to describe what I wanted Daniel to do. But it was the relationship between the right arm and left shoulder when his right foot first left the ground at the back of the ring that would allow him to do this. Sound complicated? That is why I bundled the cues together into one "packet."

In his throwing sessions on Monday and Tuesday, Daniel began with 5 full throws at submaximal effort from a static start with no reverse. Those throws were followed by 5 non-reverse throws using his full windup, then 10 full throws with a reverse. None of these throws was taken with maximal effort. We emphasized maintaining control--no fouls--and just focusing on "the packet."

Daniel typically has great concentration in the days before a major competition, and this week was no exception. Over the two days, his technique was solid on one hundred percent of his throws.

In the weight room, we stayed with 3x3 but lightened the load by five or ten percent over what he had been using the past few sessions.

Daniel Ståhl Prog 14 Speed & Power #2	14/07-31/07 2021
SESSION 1	SESSION 2
28-Jul	
REST	REST
29-Jul	
REST (Cardio)	REST
30-Jul	
MEET: Olympic Qualification	REST
31-Jul	
REST (Cardio)	MEET: Olympic Final

July 28 and 29

We traveled to Tokyo and checked into the Olympic Village on the 28th. Because we had already been in the country, we did not have to repeat the

Covid protocol, which made this an easy trip. Also, because these were rest days, we did not have to worry about what time throwers would be able to use the ring in the stadium, which can sometimes be a hassle. We arrived in town ready to go.

July 30

Daniel threw 66.12m on his first attempt in qualification. The automatic qualifying mark was 66.00m, so he was one-and-done.

Simon took a bit longer, hitting 64.18m on his third attempt, the seventh-best throw in qualification.

July 31

In the final, Daniel took the gold with a 68.90m toss in round two. Simon shocked everyone by going 67.39m in round five to take the silver medal.

In the women's shot put qualifying, Fanny threw 19.01m to make the final. Two days later, she threw 18.91m to finish seventh.

And so, we accomplished our mission.

Afterward

By the time you read this, much will have changed. In March of 2023, I retired from active coaching to take an administrative position with the Icelandic Federation. Daniel, after a difficult 2022 season, found his rhythm again under the guidance of a new coach, Staffan Jönsson, and threw 71.46m on his final attempt at the 2023 World Championships to take the gold medal. We have another book coming out which explains in detail my years with Daniel and my decision to leave coaching. I will let you read that to find out more.

In the meantime, I hope these details about the training plan we used to help Daniel win Olympic gold will help on your own journey to success.

About the Authors

Vésteinn Hafsteinsson is one of the most successful throwing coaches in history. A proud son of Selfoss, Iceland, Vésteinn competed in four Olympic Games and five World Championships as a discus thrower. After transitioning to coaching in the mid 1990's, he worked with 56 athletes from 10 different countries, most prominently Joachim Olsen of Denmark (2004 Olympic shot put silver), Gerd Kanter of Estonia (2007 World and 2008 Olympic discus gold), and Fanny Roos (2021 European Indoor shot put silver, 2023 bronze), Simon Pettersson (2021 Olympic discus silver), and Daniel Ståhl (2019 World and 2021 Olympic discus gold) of Sweden. In total, Vésteinn's athletes earned 20 medals at major international championships. He and his wife, Anna, have raised three children–Örn, Olga, and Albert–and plan to spend the next five years in Iceland, where Vésteinn will serve as Head of Elite Sports.

Dan McQuaid is a high school throwing coach and retired English teacher who lives with his immensely patient wife in the Chicago suburb of Naperville, Illinois. He has two grown stepsons and an eight-year-old grandson who regularly destroys him in driveway basketball. Dan is proud that his daughter, KC, is about to embark on her own career as a teacher, coach, and writer, though why she chose distance running after having been raised among large people with chalky hands remains a mystery. Dan and Roger Einbecker, who also contributed to this book, manage the Mcthrows.com website, through which they produce articles and webinars about the sport of throwing.

www.ingramcontent.com/pod-product-compliance
Lightning Source LLC
Chambersburg PA
CBHW051348110526
44591CB00025B/2938